# AMERICAN CARS
## OF THE
# 1950s

### BY THE AUTO EDITORS OF
### CONSUMER GUIDE®

Publications International, Ltd.

Manufactured in China.

8 7 6 5 4 3 2 1

ISBN: 1-4127-1156-8

Library of Congress Control Number: 2004113589

The images in this book were reproduced from original manufacturer brochures, advertisements, and factory photos. We thank the various manufacturers for the use of these images and for the creativity shown by the talented artists of the day.

# Table of Contents

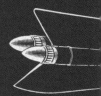

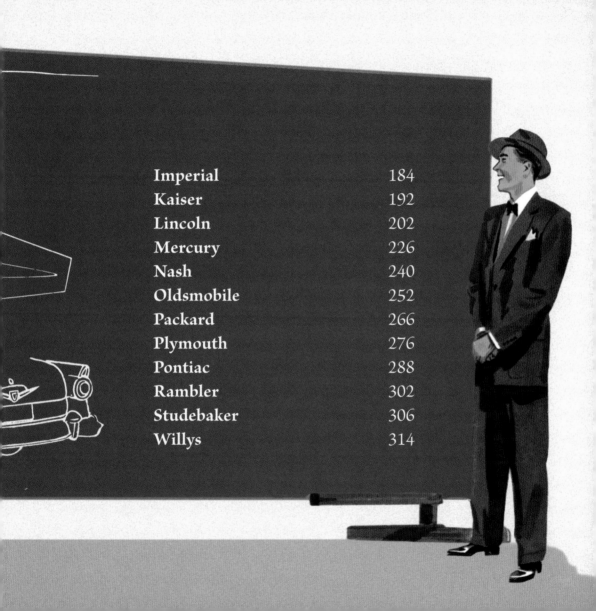

| Imperial | 184 |
| Kaiser | 192 |
| Lincoln | 202 |
| Mercury | 226 |
| Nash | 240 |
| Oldsmobile | 252 |
| Packard | 266 |
| Plymouth | 276 |
| Pontiac | 288 |
| Rambler | 302 |
| Studebaker | 306 |
| Willys | 314 |

# Foreword

Brash, finned, dripping with chrome, Detroit's cars of the 1950s reflected the spirit of the day. Born of a booming postwar economy, their bold designs echoed the nation's bright outlook. So, too, did the automakers' advertising.

*American Cars of the 1950s* celebrates this vibrant decade through its automotive ads and brochures. This is the most unique collection of this art form ever published.

Before the proliferation of color TV, or even the perfection of color photography, these stylized illustrations done with pen and paintbrush captured the glamour of the cars and the era.

Automotive literature of the 1950s did more than show potential buyers the newest products from Detroit. It presented an idyllic view of the American Dream. Relive that vision in the pages of *American Cars of the 1950s*.

# BUICK

A bold, toothy grille dominated the front view of all 1950 Buicks, while new bodies wore voluptuous fender contours. Buicks were offered in three trim levels: Special, Super, and top-line Roadmaster. Roadmasters could be distinguished by the four "VentiPorts" on their hoodsides—Specials and Supers wore only three. The Roadmaster convertible and Roadmaster Riviera models also sported a sweeping chrome side spear. Though Oldsmobile and Cadillac now offered overhead-valve V-8 power, Buick stuck with its tried-and-true "Fireball" straight-eight engines.

BUICK's THE FASHION FOR 1950

for an easy going life
.. let Dynaflow do it

Automatic transmissions were a relatively new technological breakthrough in the early Fifties. Buick's Dynaflow transmission debuted in 1948, and was standard on 1950 Roadmasters and optional on other models.

At $2981, the Roadmaster convertible was the most-expensive '50 Buick outside of the $3407 Roadmaster Estate Wagon. A $2844 Super Estate Wagon (left) was also offered. Buick named its slope-decked fastback body styles "Jetbacks" and "Sedanets." Shown below are Special two-door Sedanets.

Roadmaster Convertible

Super Riviera

Super Four-Door Sedan

Super Estate Wagon

Special Four-Door Sedan

Special Two-Door Three-Passenger Coupe

Buick's "bucktooth" grille was toned down for 1951, but the familiar "bombsight" hood ornament remained. Bumper guard "bombs" were larger, and the "Ventiport" portholes migrated from the hoodsides to the fenders. The Buick crest on the hood also served as a fresh-air inlet for the engine compartment. Trim levels stood pat with Special, Super, and Roadmaster models. Fastback body styles were quickly fading in popularity as customers clamored for pillarless hardtop models. Buick offered only one fastback model for 1951, the Super DeLuxe two-door Jetback Sedanet. Only 1500 were built. Entry-level Specials now carried the same size engine as Supers: a 263.3-cubic-inch straight eight. Roadmasters got a 320-cid straight eight.

12

A 1951 Roadmaster Riviera two-door hardtop (above) cost $3051, or $3143 with hydraulic pushbutton controls for the windows and front-seat adjustment. The 1952 Buicks appeared almost identical to the '51s, but wore very minor trim differences. Power steering was offered as a $199 option on Supers and Roadmasters.

Front and Center for 1952- BUICK

13

1903
1953

Buick celebrated its 50th anniversary in 1953 with overhead-valve V-8 power and updated styling. Ornately trimmed Roadmaster control panels could house an optional "Sonomatic" radio. The Roadmaster convertible was upstaged by the limited-production Skylark, with its rakish dipped beltline, wire wheels, and jaw-dropping $5000 price tag.

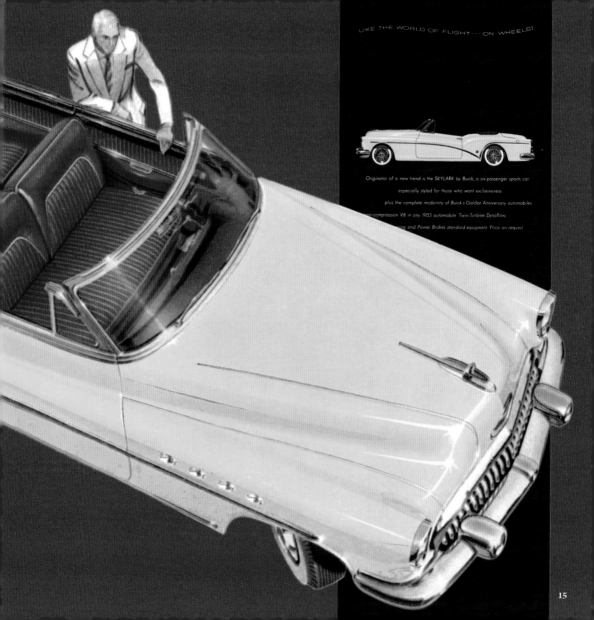

LIKE THE WORLD OF FLIGHT...ON WHEELS!

Originator of a new trend is the SKYLARK by Buick, a six-passenger sports car

especially styled for those who want exclusiveness

plus the complete modernity of Buick's Golden Anniversary automobiles

...st-compression V8 in any 1953 automobile. Twin-Turbine Dynaflow,

...ing and Power Brakes standard equipment. Price on request

## 1954 BUICK

*the beautiful buy*

All Buicks got a Panoramic wrap-around windshield for 1954. Buick also revived the Century series, a name it had not used since prewar days. Centurys were real "banker's hot rods", melding the 322-cid Roadmaster engine with the smaller Special bodies for an impressive power-to-weight ratio. The ultralimited Skylark returned, this time with wildly arched wheel openings and abbreviated rear fenders capped by chrome taillight housings. Just 836 were built.

# 1955

The horsepower race was heating up in 1955, and the new Buick pledged to be the "Hottest Buick in History." A horsepower boost and more-efficient Variable-Pitch Dynaflow transmission enhanced performance. A Dynaflow-equipped Century was clocked at 9.8 seconds in a *Motor Trend* 0-60-mph test, an impressive time for the day. Buick was at the forefront of a new styling innovation with the Riviera four-door pillarless hardtop. It came in Special or Century form, the latter with a dazzling tri-tone interior.

1955
*Buick*

Forefront of fashion
—Thrill of the year

Coming or going, the 1955 Buicks boasted
fresh styling updates that were in step
with the fashion of the era ... namely, bigger bumper bullets and more chrome.

19

# 1956
## Best Buick yet

Buicks wore a stylish facelift for 1956, with new front sheetmetal and a slightly vee'd grille. "Ventiport" portholes were now oval shaped, and all but the entry-level Special models sported four per side. The Riviera name was now used solely for hardtops. Horsepower was up again; all Buicks now used a 322-cid V-8, rated at 220 hp in the Special series and 255 hp in Supers, Centuries, and Roadmasters. Dynaflow transmission was now standard in all but the Special series, where it was a $204 option. Other options included air conditioning ($403) and power steering (standard on Super and Roadmaster; $108 extra on Century and Special).

Buick's sweepspear chrome trim made for attractive two-tone paint combinations, as displayed on the Bedford Blue and white Super Riviera hardtop sedan above. Even Buick's utilitarian wagons, such as this $2775 Special Estate wagon, boasted ample Fifties flash. The rear view shows off Buick's thick chrome taillight housings, another highlight of the 1956 facelift.

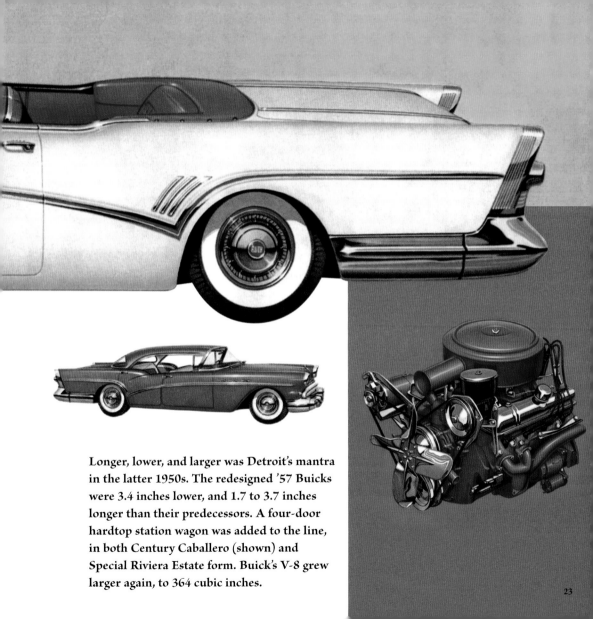

Longer, lower, and larger was Detroit's mantra in the latter 1950s. The redesigned '57 Buicks were 3.4 inches lower, and 1.7 to 3.7 inches longer than their predecessors. A four-door hardtop station wagon was added to the line, in both Century Caballero (shown) and Special Riviera Estate form. Buick's V-8 grew larger again, to 364 cubic inches.

# 1958

A "FashionAire Dynastar Grille" and dual "Vista-Vision" headlamps were among the many glittery highlights of the chrome-encrusted 1958 Buicks. A diverse array of interior configurations was offered in various trim levels. The Limited nameplate was revived as the new top-line series. Brochures claimed that the "B-58" Buick "looks and feels like flight on wheels."

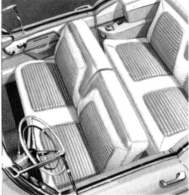

# 1959

Buick had originally intended its 1959 models to be a mere facelift of the '58s, but when Chrysler Corporation's trend-setting "Forward Look" cars stole the show in 1957, GM stylists scurried back to their drawing boards to design an all-new Buick. The resulting car was one of the lowest and sleekest bodyshells that GM had yet produced, and a definite break from Buick tradition. Radical "delta-wing" fins were matched by finlike projections over canted dual headlights at the front. The popular four-door hardtop models now had a huge wraparound rear window. Entry-level LeSabres came standard with Buick's 250-horsepower, 364-cubic-inch V-8, but all other models got a new 325-hp 401.

YOUR EYES, YOUR HEART, YOUR GOOD SENSE TELL YOU IT'S...

## THE CAR

## BUICK '59

A new class of fine cars within reach of 2 out of 3 new car buyers

**1.** Enjoy the finest ride in Buick history, finest in any car today. New Equipoise Chassis, soft, quiet, sure-footed. Quality *feet* matches quality *look* . . .

**2.** Stop with the surest-stopping, longest-wearing brakes in America today. New fin-cooled rear brakes, exclusive aluminum front brakes . . .

**3.** Admire new "classic modern" beauty. Lean, clean, low. Easy to get in, roomy to be in. Big new Vista-Panoramic windshields. New Magic-Mirror finishes. And a stunning new kind of 4-door hardtop design . . .

**4.** Feel the sense of command behind new control-center instrument panel. New constant-speed electric windshield wipers on all models.

**5.** Discover the smooth power-flow of Buick Wildcat engine and Twin-Turbine transmission*. No gears to change, no sense of power-pause. Truly automatic. Improved fuel economy . . .

**6.** Steer more easily, more surely than ever in your life with Buick's new Easy Power Steering*, best combination yet of true "road feel" and ease of control!

*OPTIONAL AT EXTRA COST ON CERTAIN MODELS.

LeSABRE . . . *the thriftiest Buick*   INVICTA . . . *the most spirited Buick*   ELECTRA . . . *the most luxurious Buick*

Buick's model roster was retitled this year with futuristic-sounding names. The lineup now ascended through LeSabre, Invicta, Electra, and Electra 225 models. The "225" suffix stood for the length of the stretched body.

Electra 225 Four-Door Riviera Hardtop

Electra Two-Door Hardtop

Electra Four-Door Sedan

Invicta Convertible

Invicta Four-Door Hardtop

Invicta Four-Door Sedan

LeSabre Convertible

LeSabre Two-Door Hardtop

LeSabre Four-Door Sedan

LeSabre Estate Wagon

# *Cadillac*

## FOR NINETEEN HUNDRED AND FIFTY

Introduced in 1949, Cadillac's overhead-valve V-8 was a trend-setting technological breakthrough that provided outstanding performance for the day. A near-stock 1950 Cadillac Series 61 hardtop coupe finished tenth overall in the 1950 24 Hours of LeMans race in France, against the world's best racing machines. One-piece windshields were a Cadillac styling innovation for the year.

Cadillacs continued to wear the tailfin humps that first sprouted in 1948. These stylistic flourishes were inspired by the twin rear stabilizers of the WWII P-38 fighter plane, and would evolve into towering appendages by the end of the decade.

# 1951

A mild 1951 facelift included larger bumper-guard "bombs" that were more integrated with the bumper, and eggcrate-patterned grille trim. At the rear, back-up lights were now integrated with the taillights. Brochures stated that "the Cadillac motor car has stood uniquely alone in the way it looks, in the way it performs, and in the prestige it bestows upon its owner."

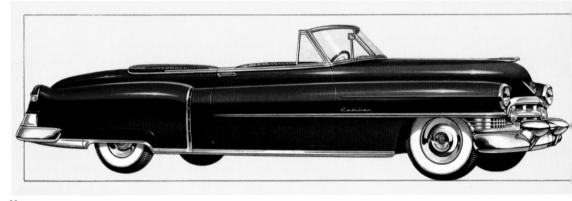

Cadillacs were the "standard of the world" in the Fifties. Perched squarely at the top of GM's corporate hierarchy, Cadillac set the benchmark for engineering, performance, and luxury. Interiors were sumptuously appointed with the latest in convenience features: Hydra-Matic automatic transmission was standard on most Cadillacs, and power seats and windows were available.

# 1952

Cadillac celebrated its 50th anniversary in 1952 by switching the "vee" emblems on the hood and decklid from chrome to gold. The addition of four-barrel carburetion helped bump the Cadillac V-8's horsepower to 190, the highest output in the industry. Dual exhaust-outlet tips now exited through the rear bumper. An "Autronic Eye" headlamp-dimming mechanism was a new option. Print advertising that displayed elegant jewelry next to the Cadillac crest was a tradition throughout the Fifties.

IT'S A "WHO'S WHO" OF THE HIGHWAY!

If you could see a line of all the distinguished persons who own and drive the Cadillac car—you would know, beyond any question, that the statement made in this headline is true. For the roster of Cadillac owners comprises a virtual listing of those known and most respected names of our day . . . men and women of recognized achievement and accomplishment . . . leaders in virtually every phase of business, of industry and of the professions. As you would expect, there is excellent reason why so many of the world's distinguished menters have found a measure meeting-ground in Cadillac. It is because they demand superlative things from their motor cars. They demand great beauty, great performance and great distinction . . . and they have come to Cadillac as naturally and in-

evitably as the night follows the day. If you hope, sometime, to find in your motor car what these many distinguished menters have found—come see us. One look and one ride—and you'll love there has never been a more wonderful year for adding your own name to the "who's who" of the highway!

*THE GOLDEN ANNIVERSARY*

*Cadillac*

STANDARD OF THE WORLD

YOUR CADILLAC DEALER

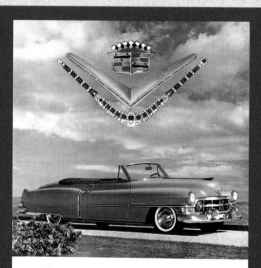

*IT'S A WONDERFUL YEAR TO MAKE THE MOVE!*

What a wonderful, wonderful year this is for a motorist to take possession of his first Cadillac car! For whoever discovers the joys of Cadillac ownership will find one of the finest engineering achievements have just made their appearance. And he'll best enjoy the perch of Cadillac ownership at a time when Cadillac's reputation and prestige are at an all-time high. So if you have been thinking of placing your order for a Cadillac—then come in and see us at your first opportunity. One ride behind the wheel will convince you—it's a wonderful year to make the move!

YOUR

*Cadillac*

DEALER

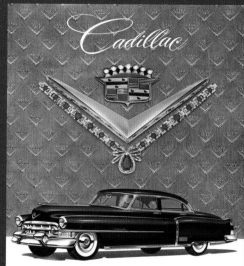

## More Eloquent Than Words!

The beautiful Cadillac crest is, beyond any question, one of the most eloquent symbols in all the world of manufactured products. In fact, it seems safe to say that no other mark of identification speaks so eloquently of the motor car that bears it . . . and of the man who owns it. It speaks of great engineering . . . of inspired design, and of experienced craftsmanship. It identifies him as a person of standing and promises only after mile of superlative motoring enjoyment . . . and it foretells year after year of dependable performance. It proclaims, in short, that here is an automobile built to the highest standards it is practical to enforce in the production of a motor car . . . And, oh, the wonderful things it says about the man behind the wheel! It identifies him as a person of standing and

achievement . . . it attests to his high regard for the comfort and safety of his fellow passengers . . . and it reveals his discerning taste and his good judgment. If you haven't as yet driven the Golden Anniversary Cadillac—we think you should come in and do so today. You might decide it's time for the Cadillac crest to tell its wonderful story about you—and your motor car!

YOUR CADILLAC DEALER

32

# 1953

"Planned obsolescence" and yearly styling changes kept consumer appetites whetted for brand-new models, but Cadillac advertising also touted long-term reliability, stating, "a Cadillac's beauty and stature are little dimmed by the miles and the years." The Detroit horsepower race was heating up, and Cadillac upped its V-8's horsepower rating from 190 to 210. Comfort was still important as well; Cadillac's first factory air-conditioning units debuted on the 1953 models.

### First Love of 20,000,000 Motorists!

The new-for-'54 Cadillacs sported slightly hooded head-light bezels up front. The Cadillac V-8's horsepower rating was upped to 230. The flagship Eldorado convertible (bottom right) wore wire wheels and ribbed trim panels on its lower rear fenders.

The redesigned Cadillacs were longer, lower, and sported a "Panoramic" wraparound windshield. With an overall length of 223.4 inches, a '54 Cadillac coupe was 27 inches longer than a contemporary Chevrolet. Protruding bumper bombs were nick-named "Dagmars" after a buxom TV personality of the day.

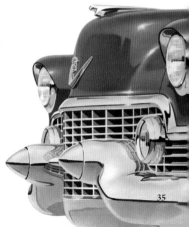

A new Cadillac was the ultimate aspirational vehicle in the Fifties, a glistening status symbol on wheels. Ownership was a brass ring of personal achievement. Cadillac was the dominant make in the luxury field, handily outselling its competitors such as Lincoln, Packard, and Chrysler. Advertising depicted polo and golf accessories, fine homes and jewelry, and regally attired models to suggest the upper-crust lifestyle of the typical Cadillac owner.

Standard equipment on all 1954 Cadillacs included Hydra-Matic transmission, power steering, electric clock, glovebox and luggage compartment lights, windshield washers, and a glareproof rearview mirror. Surprisingly, whitewall tires were an extra-cost option. Note the fresh-air vents mounted at the bottom of this coupe's doors.

Cadillac was flying high in 1955, posting a 42.7 percent production increase over the previous year. A mild facelift included rectangular parking lights in wraparound pods and a larger "eggcrate" grille pattern. The Eldorado convertible got a redesigned rear end with round taillights and sharklike tailfins. Ads called it the "Cadillac of Cadillacs." At $6286, the Eldorado was the most-expensive Cadillac outside of the $6402 limousine.

The 1956 Cadillacs
received "jet-tube"
sculpturing on their
rear fenders, a fine
grille mesh pattern,
and bumper-mounted
parking lights. The
"L"-shaped side trim
grew a more-pro-
nounced simulated
scoop on its vertical
edge. The Cadillac V-8
grew to 365 cubic
inches, and its output
was up to 285 horse-
power. Power brakes
were now standard
equipment.

1957

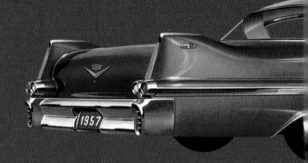

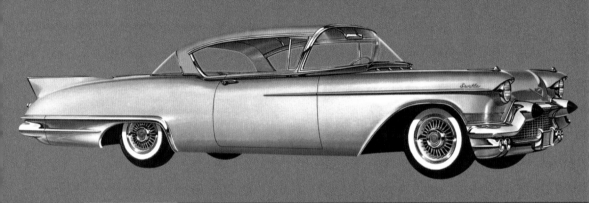

The 1957 Cadillacs were new from the ground up, and rode a new "X-frame" chassis that enabled them to sit three inches lower than before. Body restyling included chrome-tipped, bladelike fins that angled forward, and rubber-tipped bumper "bombs." Despite the new look, all of the characteristic styling hallmarks— the fins, the grille, the "Dagmars"— still said "Cadillac." Note the aluminum "Sabre" wheels on the Eldorado Seville hardtop at left.

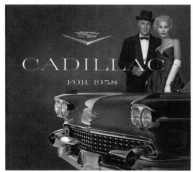

The 1958 Cadillacs gained quad headlights and a bulkier grille/bumper treatment. Air suspension was a $215 option that used compressed air-filled rubber bladders in place of coil springs. The system proved troublesome and prone to leaks. The ultraluxury Eldorado Brougham four-door hardtop (bottom right) featured a stainless-steel roof and a whopping $13,074 price tag.

# 1959

The radical design of the 1959 Cadillacs was a hurried reaction to the trendsetting 1957 Chrysler lineup. GM designers got an early look at the sweeping tailfins and airy rooflines that the rival Chrysler products were sporting, and quickly went back to their drawing boards to outdo the competition. From their gargantuan front bumpers to their tallest-ever tailfins, Cadillac's outrageous 1959 models were the pinnacle of 1950s styling excess. These baroque behemoths stretched over 18 feet from bumper to bumper and weighed around 4800 pounds. To help move that mass, the Cadillac V-8 was enlarged again, this time to 390 cubic inches. It now put out 325 horsepower in regular Cadillacs, 345 horsepower in Eldorados.

The $6233 Fleetwood Sixty Special four-door hardtop (above) wore distinctive side trim with huge faux air scoops on its rear flanks. The $7401 Eldorado Biarritz convertible (bottom left) and its Seville hardtop sibling sported thick chrome trim that ran along the rocker panels, circled up to run along the base of the fins, and stopped at the windshield pillar's base. The rest of the '59 Cadillacs wore a simple horizontal chrome trim strip.

**NEW CHEVROLET** *for* **1950**

*Smarter Styling · New Luxuries · Improved Performance*

Chevrolet got the jump on Ford with two significant "firsts" for 1950: the Bel Air hardtop coupe and Powerglide automatic transmission. Pillarless hardtops and automatic transmissions were very recent advancements that had previously been exclusive to high-priced makes such as Cadillac and Buick. A 1950 Chevrolet Bel Air started at $1741; Powerglide added $159.

Chevrolet's "stovebolt" six-cylinder engine was long in the tooth by 1950, but PowerGlide made it seem a lot newer. Buyers loved the convenience of the new transmission, but early versions were notoriously inefficient. To make up for the engine power lost to the automatic transmission, all Powerglide cars got a larger 235.5-cid engine.

# POWER*Glide*

| A | B | C |
|---|---|---|
| Start the engine | Set the Pilot Control Lever | Press the accelerator |

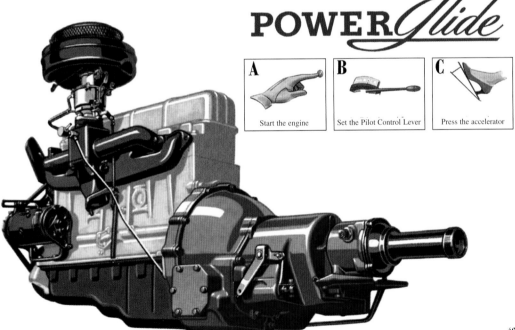

CHEVROLET FOR 1951

The 1951 facelift brought Chevrolets a cleaner grille and a "jet-styled" hood ornament. DeLuxe models were distinguished by a simple side-trim spear and chrome rear-fender gravel guard. Fastback body styles such as the Fleetline DeLuxe four-door sedan (top right) were popular in the Forties, but were falling out of fashion as the new pillarless-hardtop look took over. The bulbous, rounded look of the early Fifties would soon give way to jet-age-inspired styling. Likewise, the relatively muted colors shown here would be replaced by carnivallike pastel hues.

A toothy new grille high-
lighted the front-end view
of the '52 Chevys, while
new chrome trim freshened
the side view of DeLuxe
models. Blackwall tires were
still standard equipment,
but most buyers opted for
whitewalls. "Safety-Sight"
instrument panels grouped
gauges in front of the driver,
with a wide "waterfall"
chrome-trim panel centered
in the dash. Chevrolet's stalwart six-cylinder made 105
hp with the Powerglide
transmission.

'52

America's most beautiful low-priced car

The restyled 1953 Chevrolets came in three trim levels: the entry-level One-Fifty, midline Two-Ten, and top-line Bel Air series. Naturally, Bel Air models had the most chrome and flash.

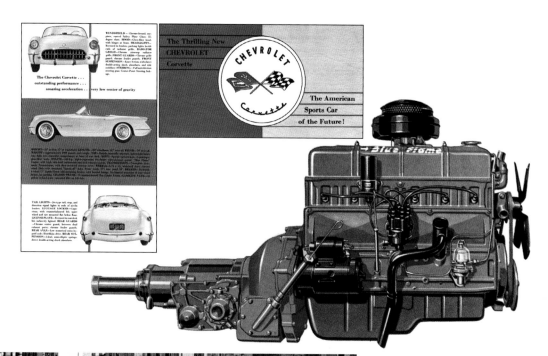

The fiberglass-bodied Corvette debuted in 1953. Though the 'Vette would go on to become America's best-loved sports car, initial sales were low. Chevrolet's "Blue Flame" six made 105 horse-power with manual transmission and 115 hp with Powerglide. Corvettes were powered by a hopped-up triple-carb version that made 150 horsepower.

53

The Corvette was little-changed for '54.
With its automatic transmission and relatively pedestrian powerplant, the Corvette
was not sporty enough for true sports car
enthusiasts, but not comfortable enough
for boulevardier types.

The 1954 Chevrolets got a new grille with wraparound parking-light pods and more teeth. Bel Airs were still the top of the line, and retained their two-tone color-insert side trim. Though they were solid, well-built vehicles, early 1950s Chevrolets were dismissed by some shoppers as an "old man's car." Chevy's reliable but antiquated six-cylinder engines were not cutting it against Ford's overhead-valve V-8s, and something needed to be done to shake off the make's stodgy image. Chevrolet executives had just the thing: An all-new, overhead-valve V-8 was in store for 1955.

# 1955

New 195-h.p.
Chevrolet
Corvette
V8

A brilliant new edition
of America's most popular
production sports car

## New Look!

## New Life!

## New Everything!

A revolutionary new engine and handsome new styling put Chevrolet back at the top in 1955. In a record Detroit year, Chevrolet led the industry with over 1.7 million cars, a new marque high and a quarter-million units better than Ford. Corvettes also got the new V-8, but sales remained sluggish—only 674 'Vettes were produced. Rarest of the regular-line '55 Chevys was the stylish Nomad two-door wagon (above center); only 7886 were built.

Chevrolet's new 265-cid small-block V-8 was an engineering landmark. Efficient, lightweight, and remarkably easy to hot rod, the new engine transformed Chevrolet's image almost overnight.

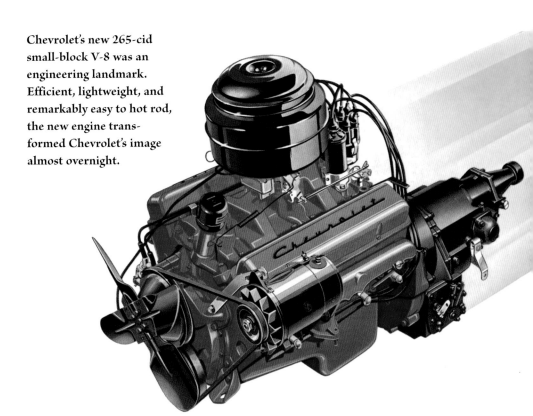

Chevrolet's new bodies featured unitized construction and a wraparound windshield. Details included a Ferrari-esque eggcrate grille, hooded headlights, and jet-age hood ornament. The well-proportioned styling of the 1955 Chevys looked especially handsome in Bel Air convertible or two-door hardtop form. Bel Airs could have a two-toned top or two-tone body sides, illustrated here by an India Ivory/Gypsy Red convertible and Coral/Shadow Gray metallic two-door hardtop.

# 1956

## Chevrolet

*offering a bigger, brighter choice than ever!*

Chevys got a full-width grille, new taillights, and other styling updates for 1956. The Chevrolet small-block V-8's reputation for performance was already well-established by the time the '56s went on sale. A preproduction 1956 Chevy set a new record for stock sedans in the Pikes Peak Hill Climb, barreling through the 12.5-mile course in 17 minutes, 24.05 seconds. Inside, "handsomely tailored" interiors differed between Two-Ten (above) and Bel Air (below) sedan models. Chevrolet offered a wide range of interior and exterior colors and trim options.

Relatively unadorned One-Fifty models (left) paled in comparison to the flashy Bel Air models (above). Eye-grabbing two-tone paint schemes in wild pastel colors were the rage in the mid Fifties, and Chevrolets boasted some of the best-looking combinations on the market.

Chevrolet advertising touted performance, proclaiming "The Hot One's Even Hotter!" The redesigned Corvette got handsome bodyside coves, a manual transmission, and more horsepower.

A NEW CORVETTE
BY CHEVROLET

Now even greater than the original in . . .

*Looks and Performance!*

# 1957

Chevrolet's substantial 1957 facelift included a mesh grille, bigger tailfins, and twin "gun-sight" hood ornaments. Bel Airs wore ribbed-aluminum "tail-feather" trim and gold-anodized trim pieces. The 1957 Chevy's iconic styling and solid engineering have made it one of history's most-celebrated cars.

Chevrolet's V8 was enlarged to 283 cubic inches for 1957. In "Super Turbo-Fire" form (above right), the 283 put out 220 horsepower. With Ramjet Fuel Injection (above left), it could put out 283 hp, or one horsepower per cubic inch. Chevy called this achievement "a milestone in American automotive history."

**FUN!**

The sporty Nomad two-door wagon body style (above) appeared for the last time in 1957. In spite of their glamour, Nomads were pricey and less practical than traditional station wagons. For every Nomad, over four times as many Bel Air Townsman four-door wagons were built.

You'll feel a very special kind of pride the day you park a new Chevrolet in your driveway. Maybe you'll even find yourself looking out the window, now and then, just for the pleasure of seeing it there. It's a beautiful sight to behold—fresh and alert, with a certain ready-to-go spirit written all over it.

And when the neighbors drop by to "look 'er over," you'll be prouder than ever. They'll see fine construction and finishing touches everywhere. They'll feel the extra solidity of Body by Fisher, and they'll see the deeper luster of Chevy's lacquer paint job.

Then they'll want a ride around the block to see if Chevrolet is as sweet, smooth and sassy as it looks. That's how people become happy Chevy owners. Stop by your Chevrolet dealer's and you'll see what we mean. . . . Chevrolet Division of General Motors, Detroit 2, Mich.

*More people drive Chevrolets than any other car.*

CHEVROLET

# You get more
## to be proud of in a Chevy!

*More beautifully built and shows it—the Bel Air Sport Coupe with Body by Fisher.*

## *full of spunk...*

but beautifully behaved...the '57 Chevy!

It doesn't just look sweet, smooth and sassy . . . it is! And you get sports car control behind the wheel . . . a solid, sure-footed feel on the road, smooth and easy response to every command.

That's why you get more of a lift out of driving a '57 Chevy. Its pep and easy handling make it fun. Safer, too. It's spacious inside, daring in design outside. But still it's a stickler for tradition, and in the grand Chevrolet manner it's known to be as trouble-free as that totem pole!

Drive a new Chevy, one with the exact power you prefer (h.p. goes up to 245*). With triple-turbine Turboglide, too, the newest and smoothest of all automatic drives (an extra-cost option). Your dealer will gladly arrange it. . . . Chevrolet Division of General Motors, Detroit 2, Michigan.

CHEVROLET

1 USA
'57 CHEVROLET

*270-h.p. high-performance V8 also available at extra cost. Also Ramjet fuel injection engines with up to 283 h.p.

*The new Bel Air 2-Door Sedan with Body by Fisher—one of 20 new Chevrolets.*

Accessories had long been an important sideline business for Detroit automakers. In the Fifties, almost every manufacturer offered an extensive selection of aftermarket add-ons. Illustrated here are Chevrolet's hand-portable spot lamp, interior courtesy lamps, and trunk lamp.

With the addition of V-8 power and the expertise of famed engineer Zora Arkus-Duntov, the Corvette blossomed into a bona fide sports car capable of competing against the world's finest. For '57, Ramjet Fuel Injection and a competition suspension package were newly optional, making the 'Vette virtually race ready right off the showroom floor.

# 1958

The '58 Chevys were longer, lower, wider, and heavier than their predecessors, and rode a new X-member frame. A new 348-cubic-inch "big-block" V-8, offering 250 to 315 hp, was optional. The model lineup was revamped and now ascended through Delray, Biscayne, Bel Air, and flagship Impala models. Station wagons now comprised a separate line of Yeoman, Brookwood, and Nomad models.

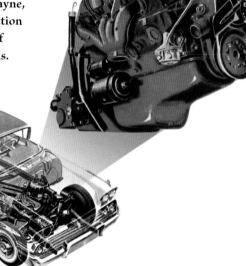

The new Chevrolet bodies featured quad head-lamps and attractively sculpted rear fenders. New Impala models supplanted the Bel Airs as the top-line Chevys. Offered only in convertible or two-door hardtop form, glitter-king Impalas had copi-ous chrome. Their exclusive trim features includ-ed triple taillights, dummy rear-fender scoops, and a faux roof scoop on hardtop models.

# CORVETTE

Corvettes also got the quad headlight treatment for 1958, along with other styling changes such as flush-mounted taillights, bulkier bumpers, and dummy air scoops. Simulated hood louvers and longitudinal chrome strips on the trunk-lid were '58-only trim details. Cockpits were redesigned with a passenger-grab handle bar, locking glovebox, and relo-cated instruments.

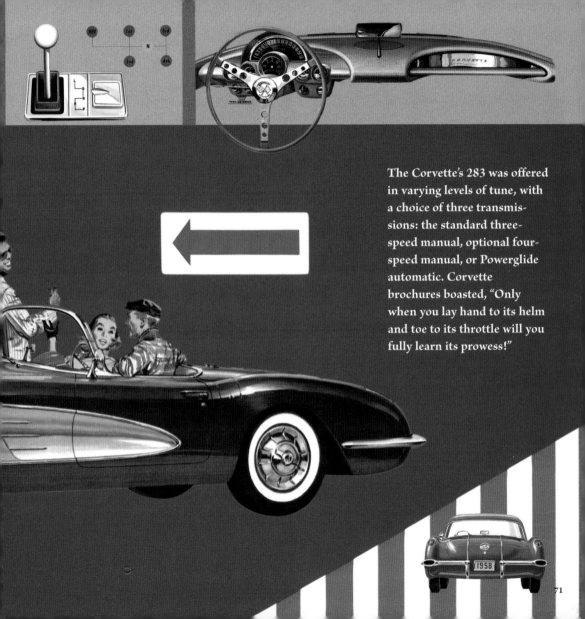

The Corvette's 283 was offered in varying levels of tune, with a choice of three transmissions: the standard three-speed manual, optional four-speed manual, or Powerglide automatic. Corvette brochures boasted, "Only when you lay hand to its helm and toe to its throttle will you fully learn its prowess!"

# 1959

For '59, Chevrolet promoted its "Magic-Mirror" acrylic lacquer finishes, available "... in an array of gem-hard colors that care for themselves." Impala interiors (left and below) were classiest.

The automotive styling race of the Fifties reached its peak at the end of the decade, as Detroit automakers tried to outdo each other with increasingly radical designs. Outlandish "bat-wing" fins and "cat-eye" taillights were the most prominent (and polarizing) elements of the 1959 Chevy's styling. Even the utilitarian wagon models looked ready for orbit—or a simple family outing at the beach. A power-retractable rear window was a $32 option.

The '59 Chevys were a bit less dramatic up front. Horizontal "nostrils" at the leading edge of the hood ducted air into the engine compartment. Note the trim differences between Biscayne (above right), Bel Air (below left), and Impala (center) models.

The Impala Sport Sedan four-door hardtop wore a novel new roofline with a U-shaped rear window and overhanging roof. Thin-pillar styling gave an airy look to all GM hardtop models for 1959.

A glittery new grille and minor trim updates distinguished the 1950 Chryslers from the all-new-for-'49 models. Wood-trimmed Town & Country models were Chrysler's low-production "glamour" vehicles in the late Forties, but the use of real wood in car bodies was quickly becoming labor- and cost-prohibitive in the Fifties. The 1950 Newport (below) was the first Town & Country hardtop, and the last "real" Town & Country.

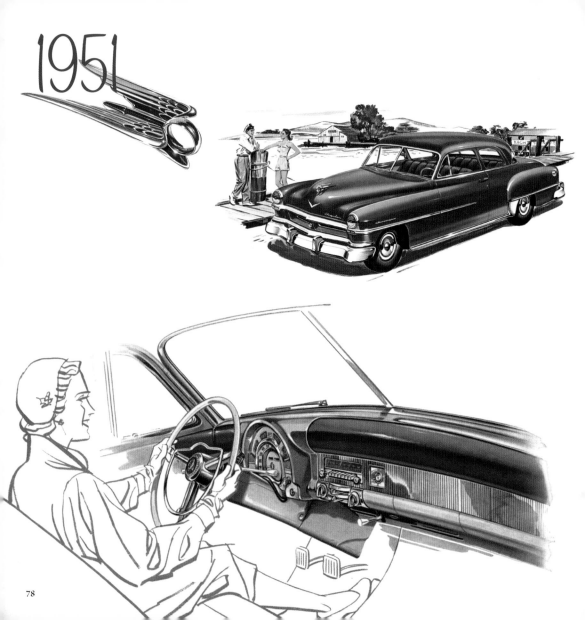

1951

A "winged-ring" hood ornament hinted that there was something special under the 1951 Chrysler's hood, and there was—Chrysler's first "Hemi" engine. Named for their hemispherical combustion chambers, the Hemi V-8s were destined to become legendary performance engines. The first Hemi put out 180 hp, a 45-horsepower jump over 1950's inline eight. Chryslers were virtually unchanged for 1952, save for taillights with integrated backup lamps.

**1953**

Restyled Chryslers wore one-piece windshields and squared-off rear ends for 1953. The model lineup ascended through Windsor, Windsor DeLuxe, New Yorker, New Yorker DeLuxe, Custom Imperial, and Crown Imperial models. Convertible tops were electrically operated, and power windows were an extra-cost option. Increased trunk capacity was part of the 1953 restyle, as was a gas-filler cap located just below the trunklid. The Windsor DeLuxe four-door sedan (below) was easily the best-selling 1953 Chrysler: 45,385 were built.

The Town & Country name was now applied to Chrysler's steel-sided station wagons. Wagons featured folding rear seats and tailgates that dropped flush with the floor for easy loading. A base Windsor four-door sedan (below) cost $2462. Chrysler's inline sixes and Hemi V-8s stood pat at 119 and 180 horsepower, respectively.

# 1954

Chryslers were freshened for '54 with revised body trim, slightly hooded headlight bezels, and an attractive new grille. PowerFlite automatic transmission, which had debuted in late '53 Imperials, was now standard on all V-8 models. Chrysler's venerable inline six-cylinder would disappear after this year.

The profile view of a Windsor DeLuxe Club Coupe (above) shows off Chrysler's "Clearbac" wraparound rear window. Note the Kelsey-Hayes wire wheels, a gorgeous but pricey $300 option, on this Canary Yellow Windsor Deluxe convertible. Chrysler interiors could be cooler for '54, thanks to newly available "Airtemp" air conditioning.

# 1955

**THE FORWARD LOOK**

Chrysler spent $100 million developing its 1955 lineup, hence its "The 100-Million-Dollar Look" advertising tagline. "The Forward Look" referred to the sleek new styling of all Chrysler products. With its progressive new designs, Chrysler began to nip at the heels of GM's styling dominance.

Chrysler's exclusive, ultrahigh-performance 300 (above) packed a 331-cid Hemi that cranked out 300 hp. Performance was blistering for the day. Chrysler ad writers boasted that the New Yorker Deluxe St. Regis hardtop , shown below in Nugget Gold and Platinum two-tone paint, was "taking America by style!"

# 1956

A handsome facelift brought more-pronounced tailfins and other styling updates to the 1956 "PowerStyle" Chryslers. Windsor models wore a three-bar grille, while New Yorkers sported a thin-bar grille pattern. Grille crests also differed between the two series. Chrysler proclaimed that its new-for-'56 pushbutton transmission controls were "a Chrysler engineering first of major importance."

Chrysler's tony Imperial models became a separate make in 1956, leaving only Windsors and New Yorkers under the Chrysler nameplate. Windsor models were powered by a 225-hp "Spitfire" V-8, while New Yorker models got a 280-hp "Firepower" Hemi V-8. Four-door hardtops, such as the Cloud White and Mediterranean Blue New Yorker shown below, launched a new body style for 1956. The eight chrome "hash marks" on the rear fenders would be a New Yorker hallmark through 1963.

Chrysler rolled out the second generation of its "Forward Look" styling on all-new-for-'57 cars, and promptly snatched the crown of design leadership away from General Motors. The sweeping tailfins, super-thin window pillars, and ultralow profile of all Chrysler products leapfrogged the competition's more-upright designs. Cleverly designed headlight pods allowed the 1957 Chryslers to wear dual or quad headlights. Quad headlamps would not be legal in all states until 1958.

The high-performance 300 models used an ascending letter suffix for each model year; 1957 models were badged 300C. A 300 convertible body style was newly available. The 300C's Hemi V-8 displaced 392 cubic inches and put out a whopping 375 horsepower with its standard dual-four-barrel carburetor setup. Despite the muscle it packed underhood, the 300C wore subdued chrome trim and was available only in monotone colors.

The '57 Chryslers' huge expanse of slab-sided sheetmetal offered a broad canvas for distinctive trim and two-tone treatments. New Yorker models (top left) wore a swatch of two-tone color in their bodyside trim; Windsor models (top right) could have a "Flight-Sweep" two-tone insert that matched the top's color. Topping the list of 1957's engineering enhancements was "Torsion-Aire Ride" suspension, which used longitudinally mounted torsion bars instead of coil springs. Horsepower crept up again: Windsor and Saratoga models got 354-cubic-inch Hemis of 285 and 295 hp, respectively, while New Yorker models came standard with a 325-hp, 394-cid Hemi.

# 1959

A more-substantial restyle marked the "lion-hearted" 1959 Chryslers. They scored close to 70,000 sales in a mild Detroit recovery. A switch from Hemis to "wedgehead" V-8s introduced a 383 with 305 hp for Windsor and 325 for Saratoga; a bigger-bore 413 gave 350 horsepower in New Yorker and 380 in the 300E.

Chrysler claimed its "mighty" 1958 models were "styled to excite—engineered to endure—priced to please." A mild facelift brought altered body trim and a different front bumper/grille, but mechanical changes were few. The major automakers weathered a dismal sales season as the nation experienced a sharp recession. Chrysler suffered more than most; production dropped from 122,273 units in model year 1957 to 63,671 in 1958.

# Continental

Ford Motor Company attempted to revive the Continental name as a stand-alone, premium luxury division with the 1956 Mark II hardtop coupe. Despite the car's timelessly elegant styling and impeccable quality, the Mark II's $9695 price tag was out of reach for most buyers. Total production for both 1956 and '57 was about 3000.

# 1958

Bearing no resemblance to the graceful Mark II, the heavily sculpted 1958 Continental Mark III came in four body styles. The convertible was costliest at $6283. Though released and promoted as a separate make, Continental Mark IIIs were basically fancier Lincolns. These behemoths defined the term "land yacht." With a wheelbase of almost 11 feet and an overall length of over 19 feet, the convertible tipped the scales at over 5000 pounds. Despite their proportions and heft, Continentals were capable of nine-second 0-60 times, thanks to an equally gargantuan V-8. The Continental's 375-hp engine displaced 430 cubic inches, the biggest in America at the time.

# DeSoto

DeSoto entered the 1950s with mildly facelifted versions of its new-for-'49 models. The Custom Sportsman (below), DeSoto's first pillarless hardtop, debuted in June 1950. All DeSotos were powered by a 236.6-cubic-inch six-cylinder that made 112 horsepower.

The long-wheelbase Suburban could carry nine passengers and plenty of luggage, with its available roof-mounted luggage rack. Both steel-bodied and woody wagons were available in the Custom series. The Custom four-door sedan was easily DeSoto's best-seller, with 72,664 produced. DeSoto radio and heater controls were mounted to the right of the steering column, while a chrome-plated, drawer-type ashtray was located in the center of the dash.

THE 1951 DE SOTO

The 1951 DeSotos got a more-sloping, rounded nose and a lower grille opening. Prominent grille "teeth" would be a DeSoto trademark through 1955. The Carry-All sedan boasted loads of cargo space with its fold-down rear seat and pass-through trunk.

Practical Chrysler Corporation honcho K.T. Keller wanted all Chrysler-produced cars, DeSotos included, to have ample head clearance so passengers could comfortably wear hats. DeSoto hubcaps bore the image of the make's namesake Spanish explorer, Hernando DeSoto.

# 1952 DE SOTO

DeSoto's big event for 1952 was its first-ever V-8. Called "FireDome," it was an overhead-valve hemi-head design—a smaller, 276.1-cubic-inch version of the brilliant Chrysler 331 introduced the previous year. Packing 160 horsepower, it put DeSoto firmly in Detroit's escalating "horsepower race." DeSoto bodies were virtually unchanged for '52, save for minor badging changes and tail-lamps with integrated back-up lights.

## DE SOTO FIRE DOME V-8 ENGINE

### 160 Horsepower

Hydraulically assisted power-steering systems became available on most American cars in the early Fifties, making low-speed maneuvers such as parallel parking much easier. DeSoto claimed that operating its power steering was "easy as dialing a telephone!" Power window lifts were another new creature comfort. Hemi V-8-powered DeSotos wore "FireDome 8" emblems on their front fenders and an "Air-Vent" scooped hood.

# 1953

DeSotos wore shapely new sheetmetal for '53, the marque's silver anniversary year. The new bodies featured curved one-piece windshield glass, wraparound rear windows, and more liberal use of chrome. These updates were the work of Virgil Exner, Chrysler's recently recruited Director of Advanced Styling. Buyers loved the power of the Hemi V-8s, but many shoppers found DeSoto styling too stodgy. DeSoto management realized that flashy, cutting-edge styling was as important as horsepower in wooing new-car buyers. More pizzazz was on the way, as Exner was gradually gaining more control over the design of all Chrysler Corporation cars.

The DeSoto model lineup was simplified for 1953: Custom and DeLuxe series names were dropped, and body styles were pared down to five six-cylinder-powered Powermasters and six FireDome V-8s, the latter including a convertible. The V-8 cars outsold the sixes by a 2-to-1 margin.

# 1954

The DeSoto V-8 was tweaked to 170 horsepower, but the big news was the midyear debut of two-speed PowerFlite, Chrysler's first fully automatic transmission. PowerFlite would be standard on many DeSotos through 1960. DeSoto promoted its 1954 models as "DeSoto Automatic," referring to PowerFlite and other convenience features that made driving easier.

A minor facelift brought DeSotos an attractive new nine-tooth grille and and revamped side trim. Flashier color choices were available, too; the FireDome V-8 convertible below wears Aztec Yellow with a red-leather-accented interior.

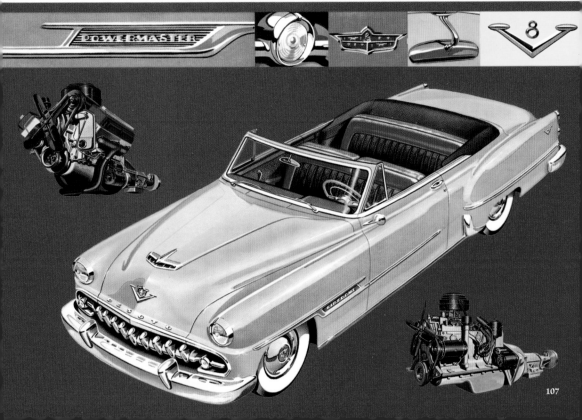

# 1955 DE SOTO

DeSoto claimed its all-new 1955 models were "styled for tomorrow!" Indeed, DeSoto's new bodies featured bolder, Exner-penned styling with a much lower silhouette. Six-cylinder models were dropped, leaving V-8 powered Firedome and Fireflite models. Interiors featured a new "gull-wing" dashboard, housing instruments under the left wing, and glovebox/radio speaker under the right. Also new on the dash was a slender gear-selector lever.

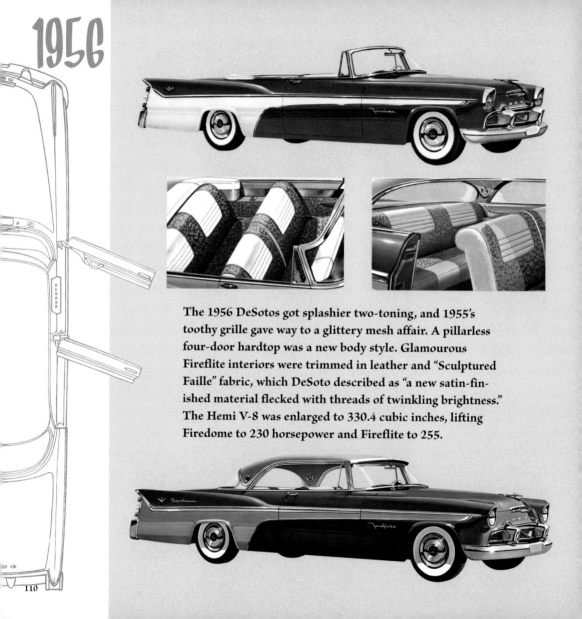

The 1956 DeSotos got splashier two-toning, and 1955's toothy grille gave way to a glittery mesh affair. A pillarless four-door hardtop was a new body style. Glamourous Fireflite interiors were trimmed in leather and "Sculptured Faille" fabric, which DeSoto described as "a new satin-finished material flecked with threads of twinkling brightness." The Hemi V-8 was enlarged to 330.4 cubic inches, lifting Firedome to 230 horsepower and Fireflite to 255.

Larger fins appeared on the
rear fenders of the 1956
DeSoto, as they did on all
Chrysler cars that year.
The new tailfins carried
distinctive "tri-tower" tail-
lamps—stacked pairs of
round red lenses separated
by a matching back-up
lamp—which would persist
through 1959.

# *1957*

The strikingly styled 1957 DeSotos were all-new for the second time in three years. The handsome cars had a dart-like profile with tri-tower taillamps attractively integrated into the soaring rear fenders, simple but pleasant side moldings, a prominent front bumper/grille, and acres more glass. DeSoto also benefited from Chrysler's corporatewide switch to torsion-bar front suspension, which made these heavyweights good handlers for their day.

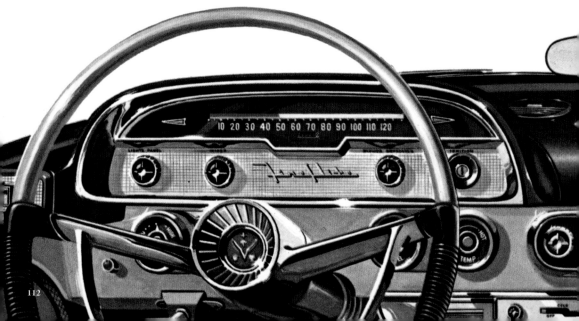

The low-slung '57 DeSotos stood just 55 inches tall. Dashboards were redesigned and featured a horizontal "Accuribbon" speedometer, dash-mounted rearview mirror, pushbutton transmission controls, and optional "safety-cushioned" dash panel.

# 1958

The 1958 DeSotos were much like the '57s save for busier grilles and trim, and standard quad headlights. DeSoto claimed that its towering tailfins of this era "added stability at speed," but that was pure propaganda. The fins did little from an aerodynamic standpoint under 80 mph. Their main purpose was to make Chrysler products stand out from the crowd—which they most definitely did. DeSotos got two new "Turboflash" wedgehead V-8 engines for '58, ranging from 280 to 355 horsepower.

# 1959

DeSotos received a busier, more-ornate look for 1959. Though the division built its two millionth car early in the year, rumors of the brand's imminent demise began cropping up. DeSoto was struggling with lackluster sales, and was threatened even from within by an upwardly mobile Dodge and a downward expansion of the Chrysler line. The DeSoto name would disappear for good after 1961.

# Dodge

The first all-new postwar Dodges debuted in 1949, and were facelifted with a fresh grille and new trim for 1950. Wayfarer, Meadowbrook, and Coronet models were available. The Coronet Diplomat (above) brought up-to-the-minute hardtop styling. The Wayfarer Sportabout convertible (below) offered open-air fun for $1727. The Wayfarer 3-passenger coupe provided cavernous trunk space.

Sleeker frontal styling was ushered in for all 1951 Dodges. The Wayfarer Sportabout—now a true convertible with roll-up windows— was in its last year. The Wayfarer 6-passenger sedan and 3-passenger coupe (right) had distinct profiles. All Dodges had "Get-Away" power, in the form of a 230-cubic-inch inline-six-cylinder engine with 103 horsepower.

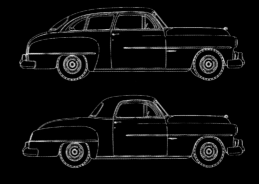

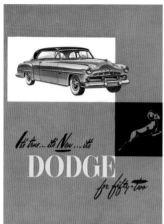

It's true... it's _New_... it's

# DODGE

_for fifty-two_

Dodges were virtually unchanged for 1952, save for new hubcaps and a splash of body color paint in the grille. Competitive makes were offering automatic transmissions, but Dodges wouldn't get one until 1954.

The $2602 Coronet Diplomat (top) remained Dodge's only pillarless hardtop model. Dodge pushed interior spaciousness and comfort, with its big "Landscape Windshield," "watchtower visibility," and "Posture-right 'Knee-Level' seats," but a growing number of shoppers wanted sleeker, lower designs.

# 1953

Dodge called its '53s "The action car for active Americans." The Wayfarer name was dropped, leaving only Meadowbrook and Coronet models. Restyled bodies were smoother and lower, but the big news was under the hood, as the hot new "Red Ram" Hemi V-8 debuted. The 140-hp, 241.3-cid "Red Ram" was essentially a scaled-down version of Chrysler's 331-cubic-inch Hemi V-8.

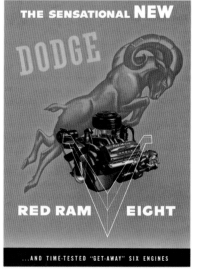

THE SENSATIONAL NEW

DODGE

RED RAM V EIGHT

...AND TIME-TESTED "GET-AWAY" SIX ENGINES

The 1953 Dodge lineup consisted of 12 models. A $2198 Coronet club coupe was the most affordable way to get Hemi V-8 power. Bucking an industry trend, the new Dodges were actually smaller than their predecessors. This hurt sales, as Americans were hungry for larger cars at the time.

# 1954

The new Hemi V-8s were fostering a new, youthful image for Dodge, helped along by mild trim updates for 1954. New Royal V-8 models displaced the Coronet as the top-line series. "Color Harmony" interiors wore Jaquard fabrics and instrument panels with "satin-tone styling." Dodge claimed its "Road Action" chassis was "engineered to give you the smoothest, steadiest ride in all of motordom!" Dodge's first fully automatic transmission, PowerFlite, debuted this year.

Despite the potent-yet-economical Hemi engines, new automatic transmission, and favorable road-test reviews, Dodge sales plummeted 48 percent in 1954. New-car shoppers wanted size and style, and Dodge needed more of both. Bigger, flashier Dodges were in the works for 1955.

Daring new, dazzling new '55 DODGE

Flair-fashioned...and alive with beauty

Dodges were all-new for 1955, with "Flair Fashion" styling and more power. Bodies featured wraparound "New Horizon" windshields, a unique split grille, and available three-tone paint. Hemi-powered models wore chrome vee badges on their hoods and decklids.

Royal interiors featured Jaquard fabric with "Cordagrain" trim. Dodges with PowerFlite automatic transmission had a dashboard-mounted gear selector called Flite Control.

# 1956

Custom Royal V-8 Four-Door Sedan

Custom Royal V-8 Convertible

Sierra V-8 Six-Passenger Station Wagon

Royal V-8 Four-Door Sedan

Coronet V-8 Convertible

Dodges were mildly revised for 1956. Tailfins were more pronounced, and revised side trim made for flashier two-tone treatments. Royals and Custom Royals now packed a 315-cubic inch Hemi V-8 that put out 218 horsepower. A high-performance D-500 package also appeared—with dual four-barrel carburetors, big valves, and dual exhausts, the D-500 engine put out 260 hp.

Coronet Six Club Sedan

Coronet Lancer V-8 Four-Door

Most mid-Fifties cars were available in an array of flowery pastel hues, but Dodge took the feminine color theme a step further in 1955 and '56. The ill-conceived La Femme was a misguided attempt at marketing a car for women. These daintily fancified Custom Royal Lancers came complete with matching rain cape, hat, and umbrella, which stowed in front-seatback compartments.

Royal Lancer V-8

Royal Lancer V-8 Four-Door

# SWEPT·WING
## '57 *Dodge*

The all-new 1957 Dodges were longer, lower, wider, and more aggressive looking, with a massive bumper/grille, lots of glass, and high-flying fins. The Hemi was again enlarged, this time to 325 cubic inches. The result, depending on compression and carburetors, was 245-310 horsepower.

Custom Royal Lancer Four-Door

Royal Lancer Four-Door

Coronet Lancer Four-Door

Custom Royal Lancer Two-Door

Royal Lancer Two-Door

Coronet Lancer Two-Door

Custom Royal Four-Door Sedan

Royal Four-Door Sedan

Coronet Four-Door Sedan

Custom Royal Lancer Convertible

Coronet Lancer Convertible

Coronet Club Sedan

Custom Sierra Four-Door Station Wagon

Sierra Four-Door Station Wagon

Suburban Two-Door Station Wagon

# 1958

A mild facelift with "Twin-Set" headlamps, a new grille/front-bumper treatment, and revised trim marked the 1958 Dodges. Dashboards featured a "Scope-Sight Speedometer", that indicated speed by a horizontally sweeping red bar.

# invitations to high adventure!

Custom Royal Lancer Convertible

Coronet Lancer Four-Door

Coronet Lancer Convertible

Coronet Lancer Two-Door

130

▲ Custom Royal Lancer Four-Door

Now in their final season, Dodge's "Red Ram" and "Super Red Ram" Hemi V-8s grew to 252 and 265 horsepower, respectively. New "Ram-Fire" wedgehead V-8s came in 350-cid size, or 361 cubic inches if the D-500 or Super D-500 option was selected. All automatic-transmission Dodges used "Push-Button TorqueFlite Drive" gear-selector controls.

Custom Sierra Four-Door Nine-Passenger Station Wagon

Royal Lancer Four-Door

▼ Royal Lancer Two-Door          ▲ Custom Royal Lancer Two-Door

▲ Custom Royal Four-Door Sedan

Coronet Four-Door Sedan V-8

With the seemingly endless array of body styles, trim levels, engine choices, color options, and accessories available from most automakers in the late Fifties, selecting a new vehicle could be a bewildering experience. Dodge's 1958 lineup consisted of 19 models in three series: Coronet, Royal, and Custom Royal. Sales plummeted this year as a result of a national recession.

Sierra Four-Door Six-Passenger Station Wagon

Suburban Two-Door Six-Passenger Station Wagon

Royal Four-Door Sedan

Coronet Club Sedan V-8

1959

The 1959 Dodges wore a rather heavy-handed facelift marked by droopy hooded headlamps and exaggerated fins above thrusting taillamps. Revised interiors could be furnished with "Swing-Out Swivel Seats," semibuckets that pivoted outward upon opening a door. The new seats were a welcome enhancement, since the ultralow bodies of the 1957-59 Dodges could make entry and egress difficult. Other gadgetry included a self-dimming "Mirror-Matic" rearview mirror.

# EDSEL

Ford Motor Company's Edsel debuted on September 4, 1957, amid glowing predictions and unprecedented hype. Awkward styling, gimmicky "advancements," and changing buyer tastes helped make it one of the biggest marketing flops in automotive history. In the end, Ford would lose about $250 million on the Edsel debacle.

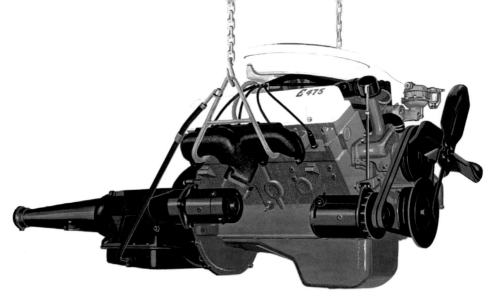

The inaugural Edsel line ascended through Ranger, Pacer, Corsair, and Citation models. All shared the controversial "horse-collar" grille. Corsair and Citation models were powered by a massive 345-horse-power, 410-cubic-inch V-8. This engine cranked out 475 lb-ft of torque, hence its E-475 monicker. Edsel interior gadgetry included a "cyclops-eye" rotating-drum speedometer and a "Teletouch Drive" automatic transmission controlled by pushbuttons.

After its dismal 1958
debut, the Edsel lineup was
reduced for '59. Pacer and
Citation models were
dropped, leaving Ranger,
Corsair, and Villager station wagon models. All
were basically reskinned
Fords. Styling was toned
down, but the characteristic vertical grille remained.
Interior patterns and trim
varied between Corsair
(left), Villager station
wagon (middle), and
Ranger (right) models.

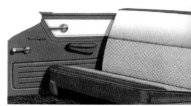

Ford called the 1959 Edsel the "finest car in the low price range," but buyers didn't seem to agree. The less-distinctive new models didn't go over any better than the garish '58 cars, and overall Edsel production plummeted to 44,891 for the model year. The Edsel nine-passenger station wagon, shown here in Velvet Maroon with Desert Tan, netted just 2971 buyers.

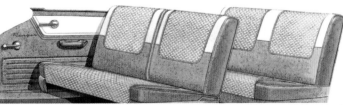

A 145-horsepower Edsel Economy inline six (top) was a no-cost option in '59 Edsel Rangers and Villager station wagons, a nod to the market's newfound awareness of fuel economy. A 200-hp Edsel Ranger V-8 (middle) and a 225-hp Edsel Express V-8 (bottom) were also available. "Mile-O-Matic Drive" automatic transmission was newly available on all three engines, while "Dual-Power Drive" automatic was exclusive to the top-line Super Express V-8. At $3072, the Corsair convertible (below) was the most expensive 1959 Edsel. It was also the rarest, with only 1343 produced.

The redesigned 1959 Edsel dashboard used a traditional gear-selector lever and optional Dial-temp heating and ventilation controls. Continued poor sales would mean the end of the Edsel marque: Production stopped in November of 1959, after a token run of just 2846 1960 models.

**An exciting new kind of car that makes history by making sense!**

The glamourous Crestliner was Ford's image-leader model. A flashy two-tone paint scheme, vinyl top, fender skirts, and full wheelcovers added pizzazz and helped Ford compete against GM's pillarless hardtop models.

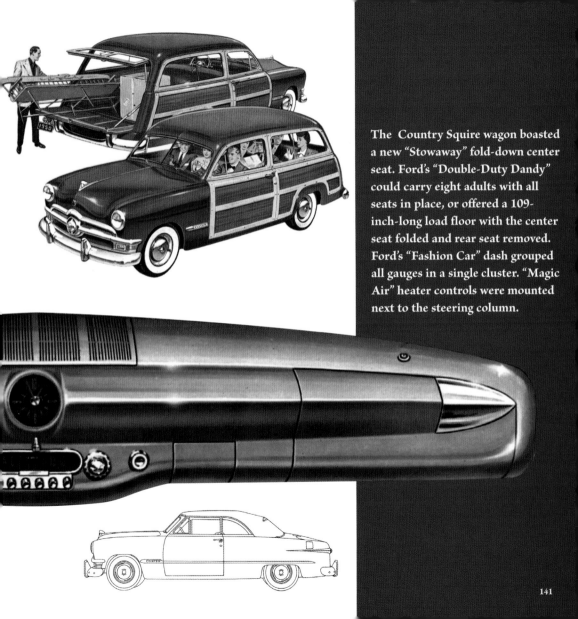

The Country Squire wagon boasted a new "Stowaway" fold-down center seat. Ford's "Double-Duty Dandy" could carry eight adults with all seats in place, or offered a 109-inch-long load floor with the center seat folded and rear seat removed. Ford's "Fashion Car" dash grouped all gauges in a single cluster. "Magic Air" heater controls were mounted next to the steering column.

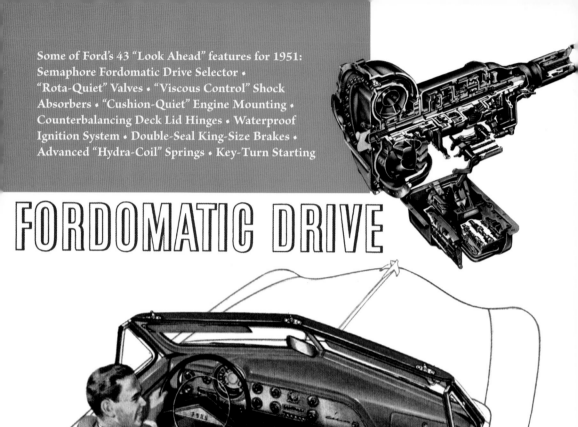

Some of Ford's 43 "Look Ahead" features for 1951:
Semaphore Fordomatic Drive Selector •
"Rota-Quiet" Valves • "Viscous Control" Shock
Absorbers • "Cushion-Quiet" Engine Mounting •
Counterbalancing Deck Lid Hinges • Waterproof
Ignition System • Double-Seal King-Size Brakes •
Advanced "Hydra-Coil" Springs • Key-Turn Starting

# FORDOMATIC DRIVE

Ford finally got a true pillarless hardtop with the new-for-'51 Victoria. The rear view of this Victoria shows off chromed "wind splits," larger taillights, and a wraparound chrome-trim strip—all styling updates for '51. The most prominent element of the 1951 facelift was the new "dual spinner" grille. Interiors were also revised, and "Fordomatic Drive" automatic transmission debuted as an extra-cost option.

143

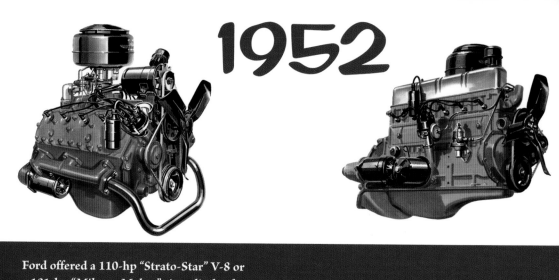

# 1952

Ford offered a 110-hp "Strato-Star" V-8 or a 101-hp "Mileage Maker" six-cylinder for '52. Redesigned interiors featured the "Flight Style Control Panel" and "Power Pivot" suspended pedals. Body trim ascended through Mainline, Customline, and Crestline levels.

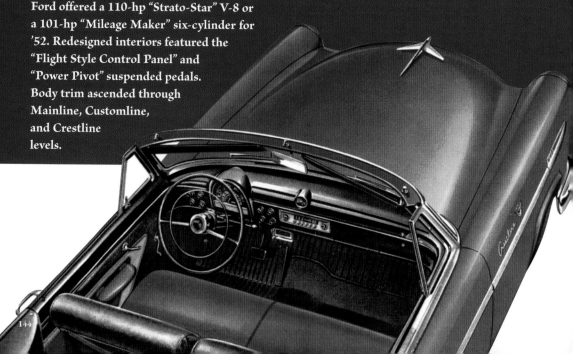

Tudor Sedan

Fordor Sedan

Fordor Sedan

Club Coupe

Business Coupe

Victoria

Ranch Wagon

Sunliner

Tudor Sedan

Country Squire

145

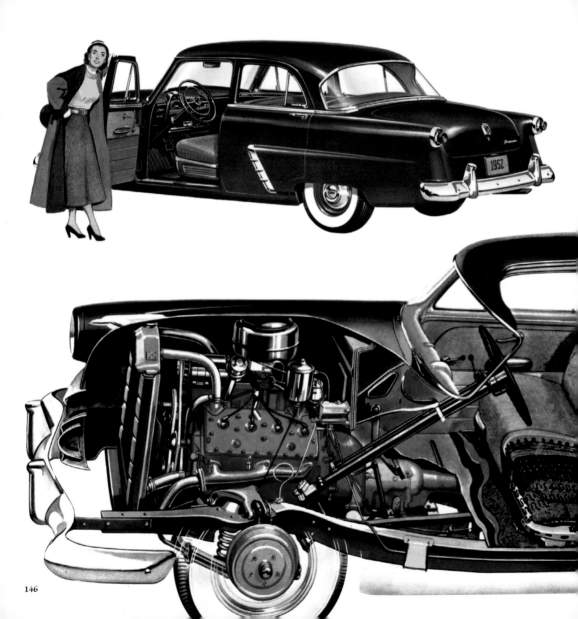

# BIG '52 FORD

GREATEST
CAR EVER
BUILT
IN THE
LOW-PRICE
FIELD

All-new styling and some tempting engineering innovations helped give Ford a leg up on the competition's carryover models in 1952. The "Big" '52 Fords were indeed a bit wider and longer than the 1949-51 models. Round taillights, a one-piece windshield, and discreet rear-fender bulges were visual highlights of the new body design, while a sturdy new "K-bar" frame helped improve overall rigidity. The gas-filler neck was now located behind a pull-down license plate holder for "Center-Fill Fueling." Suspension featured "Hydra-Coil" springs up front and "Para-Flex" leaf springs at the rear. Three transmission choices were available—Conventional, Overdrive, or Fordomatic.

*Shift to FORDOMATIC and you'll never shift again*

FORDOMATIC . . . THE FINEST, MOST VERSATILE COMPLETELY AUTOMATIC DRIVE EVER BUILT

Ford celebrated its 50th anniversary in 1953 with an attractively facelifted car. Fordomatic automatic transmission was joined at midyear by "Master Guide" power steering ($125) and power brakes ($35). The venerable flat-head V-8 would make its final appearance this year. The Customline Fordor sedan model was tops in sales.

1953 FORD

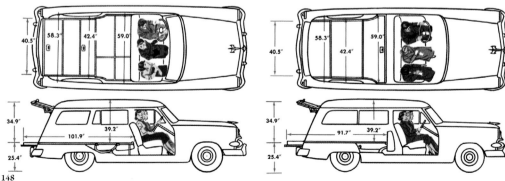

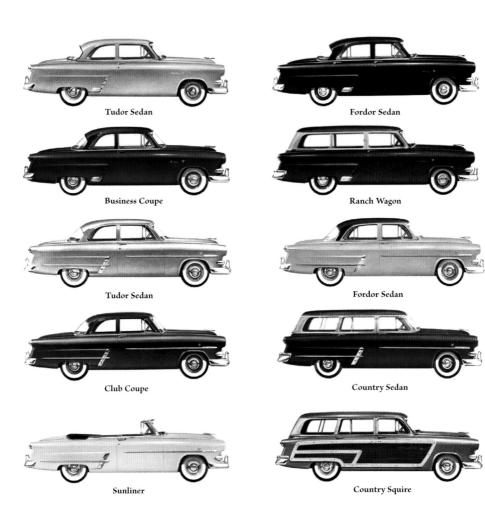

Tudor Sedan

Fordor Sedan

Business Coupe

Ranch Wagon

Tudor Sedan

Fordor Sedan

Club Coupe

Country Sedan

Sunliner

Country Squire

Crestline Victoria

# 1954

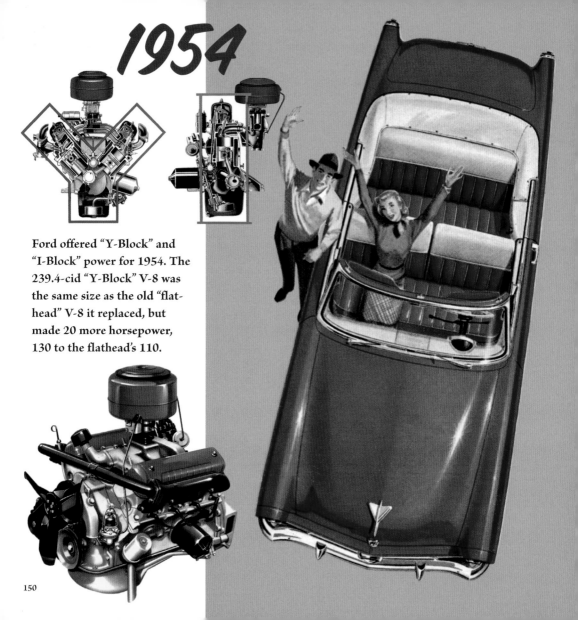

Ford offered "Y-Block" and "I-Block" power for 1954. The 239.4-cid "Y-Block" V-8 was the same size as the old "flat-head" V-8 it replaced, but made 20 more horsepower, 130 to the flathead's 110.

Ford advertising promoted the idea of a two-Ford family by suggesting the purchase of a pair of Fords instead of one more-expensive car. The "Astra-Dial" control panel used a transparent-hooded speedometer that allowed daylight to illuminate the needle and dial. Oil-pressure and generator gauges were replaced with small, red warning lights. The new Skyliner model was fitted with a green-tinted plexiglass roof panel. Advertising claimed the Skyliner provided "a freshness of view, a new gaiety and glamour, vast new areas of visibility, a whole new concept of light and luxury."

# 1955

A flashy restyle gave the '55 Fords peaked headlight bezels, small tailfins, and a wraparound windshield. Top-of-the-line Fords were now called Fairlanes, and the Crestline name was dropped. The Fairlane models' bold "checkmark" bodyside trim lent itself to attractive two-tone paint combinations, with vibrant pastel colors such as Goldenrod Yellow, Neptune Green, and Tropical Rose. Midlevel Customline models wore more-subdued chrome trim, while the entry-level Mainline models had no side trim. Ford's "Y-block" V-8 was enlarged to 272 cubic inches, and made 162 horsepower, or 182 hp with the "Power Pack" four-barrel carburetor/dual exhaust option.

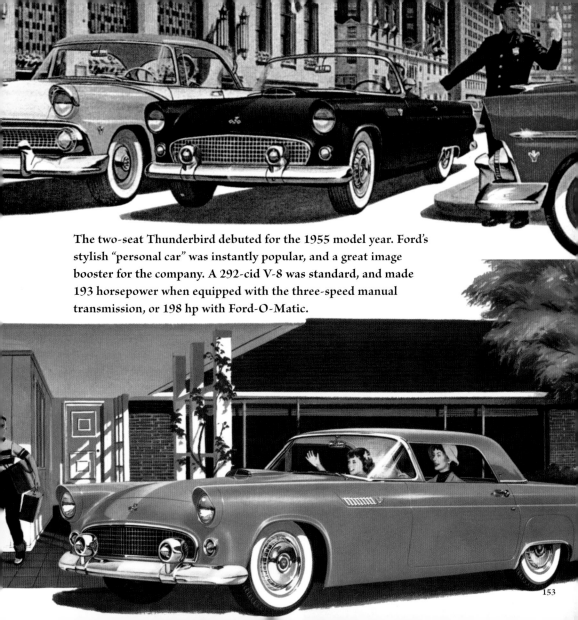

The two-seat Thunderbird debuted for the 1955 model year. Ford's stylish "personal car" was instantly popular, and a great image booster for the company. A 292-cid V-8 was standard, and made 193 horsepower when equipped with the three-speed manual transmission, or 198 hp with Ford-O-Matic.

154

With its unique "basket-handle" chrome roof trim, the Crown Victoria hardtop coupe was the flagship of the Fairlane line. For an additional $70 over the Crown Victoria's $2202 base price, buyers could choose a Plexiglass roof insert, but only 1999 Crown Vics were so equipped. Fully optioned "Astra-Dial" control panels sported three circular binnacles that housed "MagicAire" heating/ventilation controls, radio with five-station pushbutton tuning, and clock. Five different station wagon models were offered, ranging from the $2043 two-door Ranch wagon to the wood-sided Country Squire at $2392. The Country Squire's "wood" trim was actually fiberglass covered by a maple-grain transfer.

Country Squire

Eight-Passenger Country Sedan

Six-Passenger Country Sedan

Custom Ranch Wagon

Ranch Wagon

155

# 1956

Ford advertising pushed safety in 1956, though most buyers were more interested in glamour and performance— and, of course, competitive pricing. A promising young Ford salesman in Pennsylvania named Lee Iacocca concocted a novel campaign to jump-start sales: "A 56 for 56"—meaning a '56 Ford for $56 a month. The gimmick was a huge success, and Ford general manager Robert McNamara soon applied the idea nationwide. The '56 Fords wore a subtle facelift that included a wide-grate grille and horizontal parking lights in wraparound chrome pods. The top engine this year was a 312-cid V8 that made 215 hp.

The new Victoria . . . one of Ford's 18 models for '5

## You'll be safer in a '56 Ford !

For 1956, Ford announces the first major contribution to passenger and driver protection in accidents: New Lifeguard Design! It is the end result of more than two years of research by Ford in co-operation with universities, medical associations, and safety experts. It is designed to give you added protection in the areas where *the majority of serious accident injuries occur.*

You get this Lifeguard protection in a car u matched for beauty . . . with styling inspired the Ford Thunderbird. What's more, Ford bring you the sheer delight of commanding the ne 202-h.p. Thunderbird Y-8 engine*—a new smooth running, Go-packed, deep-block engine that w put fresh enthusiasm into all your driving.

*In Fordomatic Fairlane and Station Wagon models

### New Lifeguard steering wheel

Safety experts called for a wheel that would protect the driver from the steering post in an accident. The deep-center structure of Ford's new Lifeguard steering wheel provides a cushioning effect under impact.

### New Lifeguard door latches

Safety experts say that passengers are considerably safer in accidents if they stay inside the car. Ford's new Lifeguard double-grip door locks reduce the possibility of doors springing open under strain and occupants being thrown from the car.

### New Ford seat belts

Safety experts asked for belts to hold driver and passengers securely in their seats in sudden stops. Ford's optional nylon-rayon cord seat belts are solidly anchored to the steel flooring and will withstand a force of 4,000 lbs.!

### New Lifeguard padding

Safety experts recommend cushioning hard surfaces within a car to reduce hea injuries. Ford's optional Lifeguard padding on con trol panel and sun visors absorbs impacts . . . helps to guard you from injury

*Fairlane* **SUNLINER—**
Test drive the new '56 Ford with

157

# 1957

Fords received a major overhaul for 1957. Trim levels were reshuffled to comprise Custom, Custom 300, Fairlane, and Fairlane 500 models. Flashy two-tone paint was available on all. So were accessories—highlighted here are the deluxe antenna, rear-seat speaker, sports spare-wheel carrier, back-up lights, exhaust deflectors, fender shields, rocker panel trim, turbine wheel covers, bumper guards, visored full-view mirror, and "Aquamatic" windshield washer/wiper. Sales brochures touted "Giant-Grip" brakes and four-way ball-joint front suspension.

Ford's open-air roster grew this year, as the Sunliner rag-top was joined by the Skyliner retractable-hardtop convertible. Buyers chose the more-economical Sunliner over the Skyliner by a 4-to-1 margin. Ford produced a record 1.67 million cars during the model year, outselling Chevrolet. The two-seat Thunderbird entered its third and final year carrying fresh front and rear styling. Trunk length grew five inches over the '55-'56 models. Round "port-hole" windows aided visibility out of the detachable hardtop. The top engine was a super-charged 312-cubic-inch V-8 rated at 300 horsepower, but only 208 buyers selected that $500 option.

# 1958

Though the 1955-57 Thunderbirds were well-loved cars, their two-seat layout limited potential sales. Ford unveiled a redesigned four-seat Thunderbird for 1958, and sales came close to doubling. A bigger, 352-cubic-inch V-8 with 300 horsepower helped offset the added heft of the new body and chassis. The new models gained the nickname "squarebird" for their blocky shape.

ORD *PRESENTS THE NEW*
### 4-PASSENGER THUNDERBIRD
AMERICA'S MOST INDIVIDUAL CAR

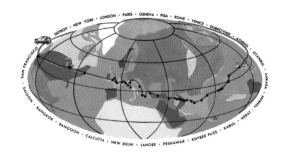

Ford boasted that its 1958 cars were "proved and approved around the world" in globe-hopping road tests. Note the differing side-trim patterns and "Styletone" two-tone paint treatments on the models pictured here. Ford's new "Interceptor Special" 332-cid V-8 was optional across the board.

Ranchero

Fairlane Club Victoria

Custom 300 Business Sedan

Fairlane Town Victoria

Custom 300 Tudor

Fairlane Town Sedan

Custom 300 Fordor

Fairlane Club Sedan

Fairlane 500 Skyliner

Nine-Passenger Country Squire

Fairlane 500 Town Victoria

Nine-Passenger Country Sedan

Fairlane 500 Club Victoria

Six-Passenger Country Sedan

Fairlane 500 Sunliner

Del Rio Ranch Wagon

Fairlane 500 Town Sedan

Fordor Ranch Wagon

Fairlane 500 Club Sedan

Ranch Wagon

163

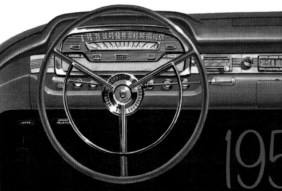

1959

Ford cars were totally restyled for
1959, with new "Safety Curved"
instrument panels. The Galaxie
line debuted at midyear, bumping
the Fairlane 500 from its perch at
the top of Ford's roster. The four-
seat Thunderbird was a continued
sales success, receiving only minor
trim changes in its sophomore year.
But under the T-Bird's hood, a
potent 430-cid V-8 with 350 horsepower was a new option. Ford was
quick to use the Thunderbird's
cachet to sell its mainline cars— all
Ford V-8s carried the Thunderbird
moniker for '59, and brochures for
the Galaxie boasted of the line's
"Thunderbird Elegance." The new
Fords netted the gold medal for
exceptional styling at the Brussels
World's Fair, and Ford produced its
50-millionth vehicle in June 1959.

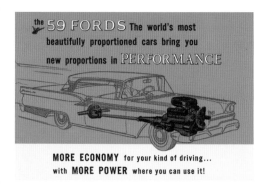

the **59 FORDS** The world's most beautifully proportioned cars bring you new proportions in **PERFORMANCE**

**MORE ECONOMY** for your kind of driving... with **MORE POWER** where you can use it!

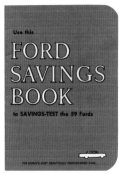

Use this

FORD SAVINGS BOOK

to SAVINGS-TEST the 59 Fords

THE WORLD'S MOST BEAUTIFULLY PROPORTIONED CARS

The Ford Savings Book listed prices for Ford, Chevrolet, and Plymouth prices, so customers could calculate how much they could save by choosing a Ford. In the book, Ford claimed that its Diamond Lustre Finish would never need waxing.

The Handcrafted Frazer

# FRAZER

The Pride of Willow Run

Joseph W. Frazer and Henry J. Kaiser met in 1945 to develop the cars that bore both of their names. Frazer had a reputation as a super salesman; Kaiser was a shipbuilding tycoon. The 1950 Frazers were identical to the 1949 models; in fact, they were merely leftover 1949 models with new serial numbers. A Frazer four-door sedan cost a substantial $2395 in standard form.

The 1951 Frazers wore a deft restyling job, with new-design front and rear fenders mated with leftover bodies from previous production runs. The Frazer would disappear after '51, as Kaiser-Frazer focused on the Kaiser line and the Henry J compact car.

# Henry J

Named for Kaiser-Frazier executive Henry J. Kaiser, the Henry J debuted in 1951 as an entry-level economy car. Standard models got a 68-horsepower inline four, while DeLuxes packed an 80-hp straight six. Initial sales were encouraging at almost 82,000 units, but demand fell off quickly. One reason was price—though a four-cylinder Henry J was indeed affordable at $1363, a full-size six-cylinder Chevrolet cost just $200 more.

169

Henry Js were sparsely equipped cars— the 1951 models lacked even a trunklid or glovebox. Armrests, turn signals, bumper guards, a radio, full hubcaps, and white-wall tires were all extra-cost accessories. For 1952, new model names were adopted: Corsair and Corsair DeLuxe. Also in 1952, Sears and Roebuck offered a mildly retrimmed version of the Henry J called the Allstate.

The 1952 facelift added a smart new full-width grille, taillights moved from the body to the fins, and nicer interiors. It wasn't enough for most shoppers—the Henry J was history after just over 1000 1954 models were sold.

Low-slung "Step-down" Hudsons hit the market in 1948, and were carried through to 1950 with little change. The "Step-down" designation referred to the cars' dropped floorpan, which was surrounded by a "Monobilt" frame structure. This unitized body construction made for a smoother ride and a lower center of gravity for better handling. Rigid frame girders also surrounded the passengers, making the "Step-down" Hudsons some of the safest cars on the road. The base engine was a 112-horsepower "Pacemaker" inline six.

# 1951

Hudsons were mildly facelifted for 1951 with a more prominent grille and revised trim. A fashionable hardtop body style, named "Hollywood," was added to the model lineup, and an automatic transmission, GM's Hydra-Matic, was newly available for $158 extra. Hudson responded to the quickening pace of the Fifties "horsepower race" with the powerful six-cylinder Hornet line.

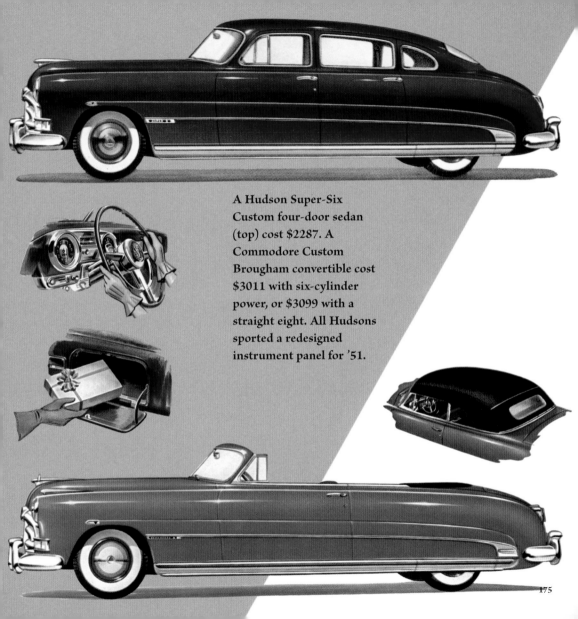

A Hudson Super-Six
Custom four-door sedan
(top) cost $2287. A
Commodore Custom
Brougham convertible cost
$3011 with six-cylinder
power, or $3099 with a
straight eight. All Hudsons
sported a redesigned
instrument panel for '51.

# 1951

Hudson's 1951 powertrain lineup included a 123-hp inline six (top) and a 128-hp inline eight (middle), but the big news was the potent Hornet six-cylinder (bottom). At 308 cubic inches, the Hornet engine was the largest L-head six ever offered. It made 145 horsepower in initial form, and was capable of far more in the hands of precision tuners. Hornets were virtually unbeatable in NASCAR races from 1952-54.

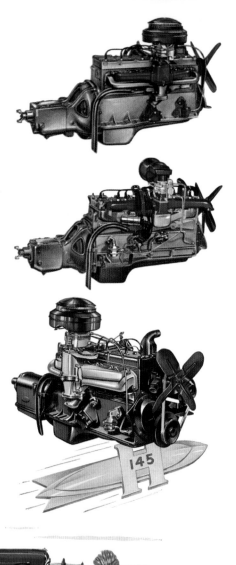

## A fabulous new HUDSON HORNET 1952 is here

...with a new, lower-priced running mate, the spectacular

## HUDSON WASP

There's a gorgeous new Hudson Hornet with Miracle H-Power, and new Hudson-Aire Hardtop Styling at standard sedan and coupe prices. This newest motor-fashion was formerly available only at premium price.

There's a spectacular new Hudson Wasp, lower-priced running mate for the Hudson Hornet, with thrilling performance in its H-127 engine!

All Hudsons have "step-down" design, proved by a million owners to provide more room, a better ride, greater safety than any other car.

### Hudson-Aire Hardtop Styling
at standard sedan and coupe prices

Hydra-Matic Drive available at extra cost on all Hudsons for '52.

Standard trim and other specifications and accessories subject to change without notice.

These brilliant new cars with a stunning new **COMMODORE** and a thrifty new **PACEMAKER** make the most exciting array of values in all Hudson history!

Hudson received only modest alterations to grille and exterior trim for 1952. The old Super Six series was supplanted by the Wasp, built on the baseline Pacemaker platform but powered by the larger Commodore Six engine. Hudson couldn't afford to develop a V-8 engine, but the sixes could get a horsepower boost via a "Twin-H Power" dual-carburetor package that appeared midyear.

**HUDSON Monobilt Body-and-Frame\*** with "Step-Down" Design
...for longest life and greatest safety

*Trade-mark and patents pending.*

Try it yourself to prove HUDSON qualities!

The Spectacular New Hudson WASP
HOLLYWOOD

You can see the style ... come try the power!

177

# 1953

The full-size Hudson lineup
was trimmed to three series
for 1953: Wasp, Super Wasp,
and Hornet. The old
Commodore Eight's straight-
eight engine was also
dropped, leaving only six-
cylinder powerplants. The
Hudson Jet compact car
(below) debuted in two- or
four-door sedan body styles,
each packing a 104-hp,
202-cid six.

As innovative as the Hudson "Step-down" models were, their unibody construction made styling facelifts difficult. Sales began to plummet as Hudson was forced to offer the same old styling next to more up-to-date cars from competing manufacturers. The Hudson Jet also floundered in the marketplace, due to its relatively high sticker price and a lukewarm demand for small cars. By the end of the 1953 model year, Hudson had lost a staggering $10.5 million.

# 1954

# NEW LOW PRICE
## FOR THE NATIONAL CHAMPION

**Winner of more stock-car events than all other makes combined!**

"Family cars like those you buy from dealers, compete in stock-car events throughout the U. S. Records show which is safest, most roadable, durable. These records show it's Hudson—with no other make even close," says Frank Mundy, AAA champion, shown in his winning Hornet.

Despite the company's dwindling fortunes, Hudson brought out extensively facelifted "Step-down" models for 1954. New body sheetmetal and one-piece windshields lent a more contemporary appearance, but sales still sputtered.

Hudson Hornet Special Club Coupe. Also available in Four-Door Sedan and Club Sedan.

# New HUDSON HORNET SPECIAL

Now! You can own the fabulous champion of the U. S. stock-car tracks . . . at a new low price. It's the Hudson Hornet Special. It has a Hornet engine, full Hornet size, gives you full championship performance.

It gives you a silk-smooth, rock-solid, safe ride due to its low center of gravity . . . the result of Hudson's exclusive "step-down" design. It's the safest car built; and one of the most comfortable.

The Hornet Special gives you Flight-Line Styling, luxury far beyond its low price. Nothing, save the Hornet itself, can equal it. Your Hudson dealer will gladly let you drive the new Hornet Special. Call him soon.

THE
**HORNETS**
THE
**WASPS**
THE
**JETS**

## HUDSON DIVISION OF AMERICAN MOTORS

Standard trim and other specifications and accessories subject to change without notice.

Beautiful performers — new Hudson Hornet Hollywood hardtop (available with V-8 or Championship Six engine) and Star Water-Ski Performers of Cypress Gardens, Winter Haven, Florida.

## Beautiful, new Hudsons by American Motors give you all these extras . . . at no extra cost!

Extra room, ride, vision, and safety . . . top big list of features found nowhere else at any price!

**Hudson seats are wider** than those in any other car at any price — nearly six inches of extra room in many cases! Headroom is again the best in any car at any price — three inches more than in some of the most expensive cars built today! See it for yourself.

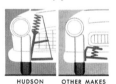

HUDSON     OTHER MAKES

**Extra-smooth, steady ride.** Hudson brings you American Motors' exclusive, new Deep Coil Ride — at no extra cost. Long coil springs, with three times ordinary cushioning power, slanted outward for new anti-sway safety — for smoother riding, easier handling.

**Widest wrap-around windshield** — you get extra vision-area in Hudson — easier, more relaxed driving. The widest wrap-around windshield in the business (completely free from distortion anywhere) teams up with a new lowered hood to give you perfect forward vision. Hudson fenders are raised to help guide you in tight spots and in parking.

HUDSON     OTHER MAKES

**Extra safety, longer car life** with American Motors' exclusive Double Strength Single Unit car construction — rattleproof, twice as strong, twice as rigid, twice as safe as other bolted-together bodies and frames. Keeps Hudson like new longer — makes it a better trade-in.

Hudson Hornet · Wasp · Rambler · Metropolitan

**Products of American Motors**

See **"Disneyland,"** great new all-family show, ABC-TV network. Check TV listings for time and station.

Hudson merged with Nash-Kelvinator on May 1, 1954, thus creating a new automaker called American Motors Corporation. The 1955 Hudsons were basically restyled Nashes, with distinct trim and an eggcrate grille.

# 1956

Hudsons got available V-8 power and bizarre "V-Line Styling" for 1956. The V-8 was available only in the top-line Hornet V-8 series, which consisted of three models: the Super four-door sedan, Custom four-door sedan, and Custom Hollywood hardtop coupe. The awkward facelift didn't appeal to many shoppers, and sales continued their downward slide; just 10,671 full-size Hudsons were sold, and the nameplate's future was in doubt.

The '57 Hudsons wore mildly reshuffled trim and slightly taller, body-color fins. Prices were lower and a new, more-powerful V-8 was underhood, but neither helped sales, and the Hudson name was dropped.

# IMPERIAL

Imperial ceased to be Chrysler's top luxury model and became a distinct make in 1955. Power was provided by Chrysler's 331-cid Hemi V-8. Unique fendertop-mounted taillights and a distinctive split grille set Imperials apart from their Chrysler kin, though not enough for many luxury-car shoppers of the Fifties. Ad copy claimed that the Imperial was designed "... for the man who doesn't seek prestige because he already has it."

For 1956, Imperials sprouted modest fins and new bodyside chrome trim strips that terminated neatly into wedge-shaped back-up lamps. Pushbutton controls were connected to a PowerFlite automatic transmission. All '56 Imperials carried a new 354-cid FirePower V-8 with the efficient hemihead design of its 331-cid predecessor. A "Highway Hi-Fi" dash-mounted record player was a new option.

185

# 1957

Like other Chrysler products, Imperial was all-new for '57, with large tailfins, an airy roofline, and a full-width grille. The Imperial line was expanded from one series to three by adding more elaborately trimmed Crown and LeBaron versions.

Imperials were mildly retrimmed for 1958, with a simpler grille pattern and a heftier front bumper with round parking lights. An Imperial Crown Southampton hardtop sedan tipped the scales at close to 5000 pounds. Overall Imperial production tumbled by half from 1957, to 16,133 cars.

1959

For 1959, Imperials received a more-extensive facelift, highlighted by a toothy grille and broad brush-finished appliqués on the lower rear flanks. An optional Silvercrest Landau Roof option trimmed the rear canopy in a textured Scotch grain finish.

As at other Chrysler divisions, Imperial switched from Hemi to wedgehead V-8s; a new 350-hp, 413-cid unit shared with 1959 Chrysler New Yorkers. It provided performance comparable to the Hemi, but was easier to build and maintain.

Drivers used an instrument-panel-mounted dial to set driving speed with Imperial's Auto-Pilot cruise-control system. Swivel seats were activated by a lever on the seat frame. Chrysler stuck with pastel colors for a little longer than some U.S. automakers; this Crown Southampton two-door wears Persian Pink.

Total Imperial production inched up to about 17,000 for 1959, but only 555 were Imperial Crown convertibles. Brochures claimed that Imperial interior leathers "retain their deep true colors for years— age simply enhances their burnished beauty."

The unique Kaiser Traveler utility sedan was a precursor to the modern-day hatchback. A drop-down trunk/tailgate and flip-up rear-window hatch gave access to a 10-foot cargo space that Kaiser claimed could haul a double bed. Other 1950 Kaiser models included the $2195 DeLuxe four-door sedan and $3195 convertible sedan.

# 1951

Looking unlike any other car of its day, the totally redesigned 1951 Kaiser boasted 700 square inches more glass than its nearest competitor and a lower beltline than any Detroit car offered through 1956. "Anatomic Design" features included thin windshield pillars for good visibility, and a padded dashboard panel.

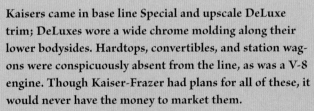

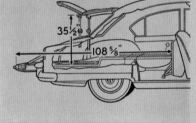

Kaisers came in base line Special and upscale DeLuxe trim; DeLuxes wore a wide chrome molding along their lower bodysides. Hardtops, convertibles, and station wagons were conspicuously absent from the line, as was a V-8 engine. Though Kaiser-Frazer had plans for all of these, it would never have the money to market them.

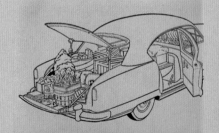

The Traveler utility sedan concept was carried over to the new Kaiser body design. Wood skid strips helped facilitate the loading and unloading of cargo. The spare tire was tucked into a well under the load floor. The Traveler's rear license plate was mounted on a special swing-down bracket so it would be visible when the tailgate was open.

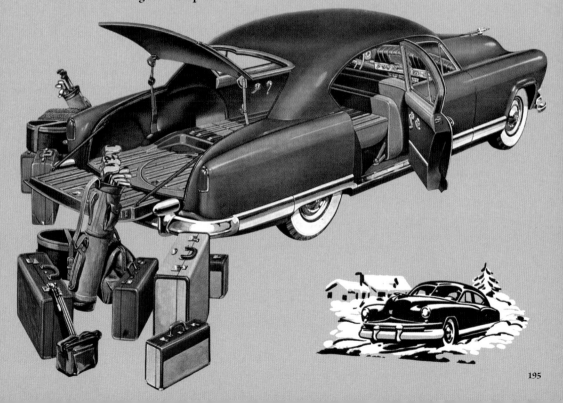

The Kaiser "Supersonic High-Torque Engine" was a 226-cubic-inch inline six-cylinder originally developed for industrial use. It made 115 hp for 1951. Kaiser claimed that its "new cushion-lined spring suspension, improved airplane-type shock absorbers and new perfect-balance engine mounting" combined to give "Flying Shadow Ride."

Kaiser-Frazer made automotive safety a central part of its sales pitch. The '52 Kaiser brochure claimed Kaisers had the "world's safest front seat!" with "Seven-Point Protection": Narrow windshield corner posts, a "Safety-Mounted" one-piece windshield, full-length padded instrument panel, right-hand emergency brake handle, recessed instruments, extra leg room, and "Safety-Posture" front-seat braces.

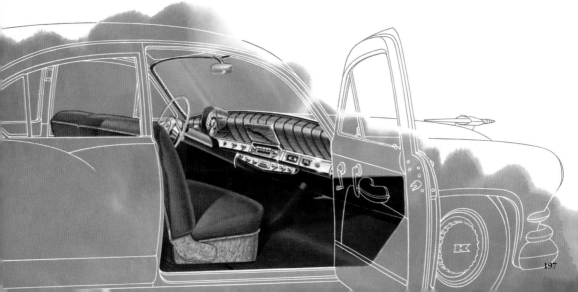

Kaiser-Frazer offered an unusually wide range of paint, trim, and upholstery variations to add appeal to its limited roster of body styles. The eye-grabbing hues and patterns were the work of "color engineer" Carleton Spencer, who took some initial cues from research on home interiors done by *House and Garden* magazine. Kaiser Manhattans (below left) and DeLuxes (below right) wore wild embossed vinyl trim that mimicked the look of alligator hide.

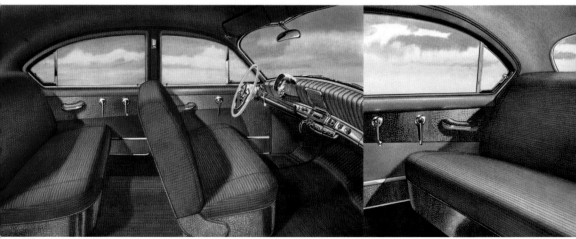

# 1953

GET ON

EASIEST ST.

Kaisers were little-changed for 1953, as the company struggled with dwindling sales and a lack of development capital. Advertising claimed the Kaiser was "The World's First Safety-First Car!" For the special-edition "Hardtop" Dragon, Kaiser rolled out one of its wildest interiors yet, a dazzling combination of deep-embossed "Bambu" vinyl and "Laguna" patterned cloth.

199

# '54 Kaiser

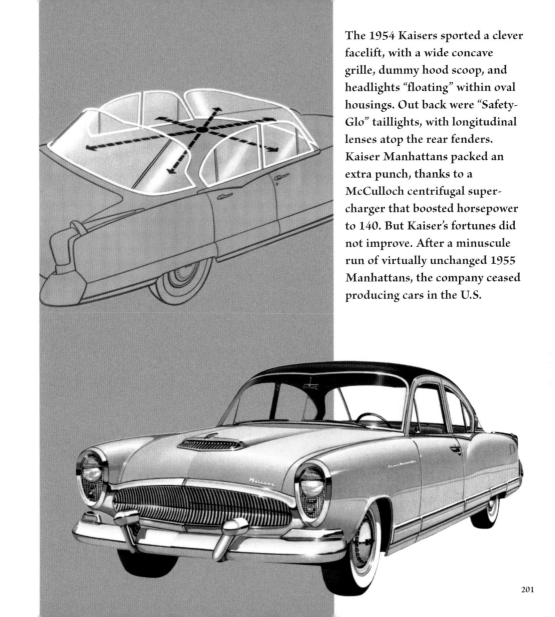

The 1954 Kaisers sported a clever facelift, with a wide concave grille, dummy hood scoop, and headlights "floating" within oval housings. Out back were "Safety-Glo" taillights, with longitudinal lenses atop the rear fenders. Kaiser Manhattans packed an extra punch, thanks to a McCulloch centrifugal supercharger that boosted horsepower to 140. But Kaiser's fortunes did not improve. After a minuscule run of virtually unchanged 1955 Manhattans, the company ceased producing cars in the U.S.

# 1950

## *Lincoln*

Lincoln's first new postwar cars debuted in 1949, and continued for the next two years with no major alteration. Their rounded bodies featured unique recessed headlights and taillights. Motivation came from Ford Motor Company's largest V-8, a 337-cubic-inch unit good for 152 horsepower—eight fewer than archrival Cadillac's 331-cid overhead-valve V-8. A self-shifting Hydra-Matic transmission, sourced from General Motors, arrived as a new 1950 option.

Rear-hinged doors gave access to a "sofa-wide" rear seat. Air conditioning was still a few years off, but 1950 Lincolns offered a "Comfort-Flo" ventilating system for "... a luxurious supply of healthful, country-fresh air."

As in 1949-50, the 1951 Lincoln line was divided into three base models and four upmarket Cosmopolitan models. The $2553 base model Sport Sedan shown here was Lincoln's best-seller, with a production run of 12,279. Extended rear fenders and a modernized rear window were '51 styling updates.

*Lincoln* ... nothing could be finer

205

# 1952

Lincolns were completely new for '52, with cutting-edge design and engineering throughout. Underhood was Lincoln's first overhead-valve V-8, a 318 cubic-incher good for 160 hp. It was standard on all models. Crisp, stylish bodies featured a one-piece windshield and an integrated front bumper/grille. A new Capri series displaced the Cosmopolitan models as Lincoln's flagship line. The new Lincolns proved their mettle by sweeping the first-through fourth-place finishes in the stock-car class of the 1952 *Carrera Panamericana* Mexican road race.

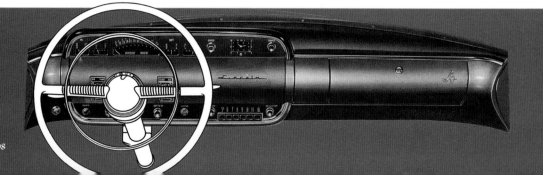

There was no fuel-filler door to mar the smooth lines of Lincoln's rear fenders—the gas cap was hidden behind a swing-down license plate holder. Lincoln offered just five models for 1952: the Cosmopolitan four-door sedan and Sport hardtop coupe, and the Capri four-door sedan, Sport hardtop coupe, and convertible. Lincoln was a little late in fielding its own version of the popular pillar-less hardtop body style—rivals Cadillac and Oldsmobile started the trend with their 1949 models. Lincoln's fresh '52 models erased that competitive deficit, with understated styling that was every bit as contemporary as GM's.

1953

Other than revised trim and a one-piece rear window, Lincoln exterior styling did not change for 1953. Underhood, the V-8 was tweaked to 205 horsepower via higher compression and a four-barrel carburetor. A 0-60-mph sprint took about 12 seconds, on the way to a top speed of around 110— very fast for the day. Inside, power options abounded, with power steering, power brakes, and an industry-first electric four-way power seat.

# 1954

The 1954 Lincoln retained the 1952-53 body with numerous trim changes. The bumper grille took on a bolder "toothy" look, and side trim was noticeably revised via a higher-mounted, full-length chrome-trim spear. The rarest and most-expensive model was the Capri convertible, with a production run of 1951 and a $4031 starting price. It was the first Lincoln of the Fifties with a base price over $4000. Not surprisingly, Lincoln played up its dominant *Carrera Panamericana* performances in advertising.

THE GROWING TREND TO LINCOLN

## How to know the story on fine-car performance

OF COURSE, your eyes tell you most of the styling story. And the new lines, the new colors and fabrics in Lincoln clearly mark it as *the* fine car designed for modern living. But you must do two things to appreciate Lincoln's superlative performance.

*One*—consider the record. Lincoln for two years straight won 1st, 2nd, 3rd and 4th place over all stock cars in the Mexican Pan-American Road Race. 1,912 twisting, tortuous miles of the most exacting test of automotive performance ever devised by man.

*Two* — drive the new Lincoln yourself.

You must feel the sureness with which Lincoln takes corners because of ball-joint front wheel suspension, found in no other fine car. You must touch toe to the accelerator to experience the *extra* automatic surge you get from Lincoln's new 4-barrel carburetor. And then you must try the safe, velvet-smooth stops with Lincoln's new giant-sized brakes.

Finally, accept this as a cordial invitation from your dealer to try the new Lincoln or the Lincoln Capri. Our forecast: Lincoln will be *your* car from that day on.

*LINCOLN DIVISION • FORD MOTOR COMPANY*

### NEW 1954
# LINCOLN
DESIGNED FOR MODERN LIVING-
POWERED FOR MODERN DRIVING

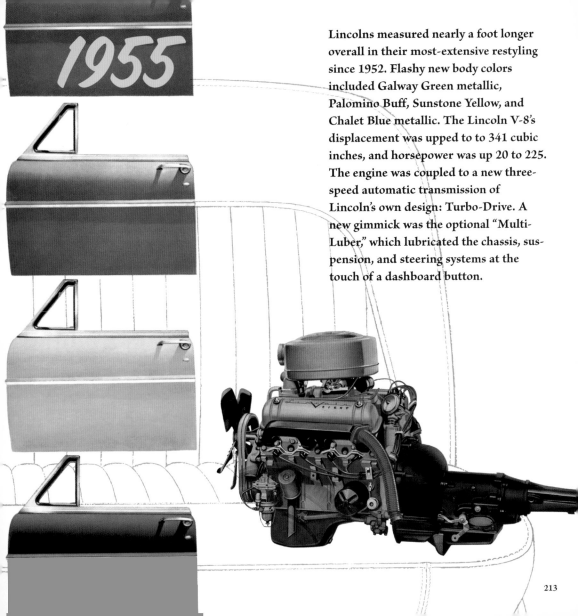

**1955**

Lincolns measured nearly a foot longer overall in their most-extensive restyling since 1952. Flashy new body colors included Galway Green metallic, Palomino Buff, Sunstone Yellow, and Chalet Blue metallic. The Lincoln V-8's displacement was upped to to 341 cubic inches, and horsepower was up 20 to 225. The engine was coupled to a new three-speed automatic transmission of Lincoln's own design: Turbo-Drive. A new gimmick was the optional "Multi-Luber," which lubricated the chassis, suspension, and steering systems at the touch of a dashboard button.

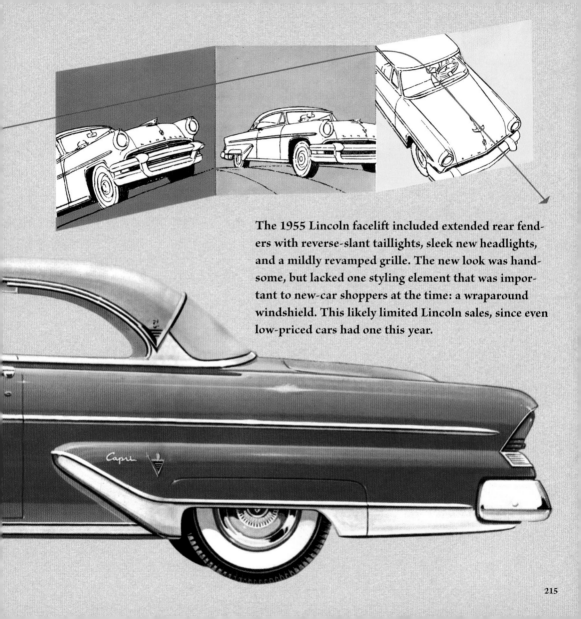

The 1955 Lincoln facelift included extended rear fenders with reverse-slant taillights, sleek new headlights, and a mildly revamped grille. The new look was handsome, but lacked one styling element that was important to new-car shoppers at the time: a wraparound windshield. This likely limited Lincoln sales, since even low-priced cars had one this year.

Capri

# 1956

Not only did the 1956 Lincoln get a wraparound windshield, it was the biggest in the industry—part of a massive redesign. The new lineup consisted of two-door hardtops and four-door sedans in Capri or uplevel Premiere trim, plus a Premiere convertible. A custom spotlight with integral mirror, automatic headlight-dimmer control, windshield washers, and a visored outside rearview mirror were some of the available accessories.

Dazzling Lincoln interiors were well-appointed, with sumptuous upholstery and plenty of power accessories. The Lincoln V-8's displacement was enlarged from 341 to 368 cubic inches, upping horsepower from 225 to 285. The Premiere convertible was the heaviest and priciest 1956 Lincoln, with a curb weight of 4452 pounds and a starting price of $4747.

# 1957

Bolder, slightly canted tailfins highlighted Lincoln's 1957 facelift. A new "Quadra-Lite" front ensemble held regular headlamps and smaller road lamps activated by a separate switch. A higher compression ratio helped bump the 368-cid V-8's horsepower rating up 15 to 300. All Lincolns got a padded dash, and power brakes became standard in Premiere models.

1958

Lincoln's new 1958 models were longer, lower, and wider, in a year when even luxury-car buyers were starting to think about a more-sensible size. As a result, model-year production tumbled. At the bottom of this avalanche was a square-lined unibody giant on a 131-inch wheelbase stretching six inches longer overall than the 1957 Lincoln. It was easily recognized, for there was nothing else like it: heavily sculpted sides, a wide grille flanked by quad headlamps in garish slanted recesses, and gigantic flared bumpers. Under a hood not much smaller than a Ping-Pong table was 1958's largest passenger-car engine: a new big-block 430-cid V-8 making 375 horsepower.

# 1959

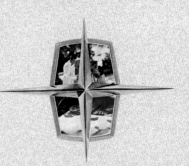

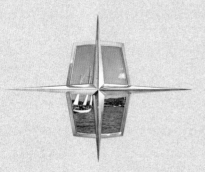

The Continental name was absorbed back into the Lincoln line in 1959, after Ford Motor Company attempted to establish it as a separate make in 1956-58. Continental Mark IVs were the new premium Lincoln series, followed by Premiere and base models. Styling on all Lincolns was revised with new grille, bumper and taillight treatments, and bodyside sculpting that was extended into the front doors. Defying recent trends, Lincoln's 430-cid V-8 was detuned to drop horsepower from 375 to 350.

# MERCURY

The 1950 Mercurys were largely carryovers from the 1949 model year, save for some trim updates. Mercury's 255-cid flat-head V-8, with an "Econo-O-Miser" carburetor, delivered 110 horsepower— 10 more than Ford's V-8. The curva-ceous styling of these "bathtub" Mercuries made them a favorite canvas of Fifties customizers, who swapped trim pieces, "chopped" tops, and lowered suspensions to personalize their cars.

# 1951

Mercurys were modernized with longer rear fenders, a bolder grille, and other trim updates. Sedan and coupe models got a larger, more up-to-date rear window. The $2530 "woody" station wagon was the priciest model, followed by the $2380 convertible and the $2127 vinyl-topped Monterey coupe. Merc-O-Matic automatic transmission, an extra-cost option, was new this year.

# 1952

Pillarless hardtop models were added to the Mercury line with the redesigned '52 models. Chrome trim on Monterey interiors mimicked the exterior-trim spear treatment.

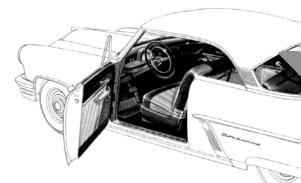

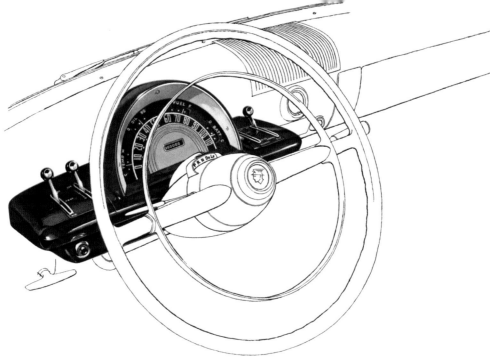

Mercury's "quik-sight" instrument panel grouped all readouts in a half-circle display. Merc-O-Matic transmission was a popular option. Outside, a "Mono-pane" windshield, wraparound rear window, and slab-sided fenders with squared and flared fender openings gave the new Mercury bodies a cutting-edge appearance. A chrome-trimmed "jet-scoop" hood covered covered Mercury's flathead V-8, which now cranked out 125 hp thanks to higher compression.

# 1953

A mild retrimming brought Mercurys full-length bodyside-trim spears and bullet-shaped front bumper guards. The Mercury model lineup was split into two distinct series— Custom and Monterey. Ford Motor Company's 40-millionth vehicle rolled off the assembly line this year— a Siren Red Monterey convertible.

# 1954

Modern overhead-valve V-8 power and ball-joint front suspension were the significant engineering advancements at Mercury for 1954. The new engine was a larger version of Ford's "Y-Block" V-8. Mercury's "Twin Tornado" combustion chambers, four-barrel carburetor, and "Power Charge" intake manifold helped boost horsepower by 36 over the outgoing "flathead," to 161 hp. Bodies were updated with a new grille and wraparound taillights.

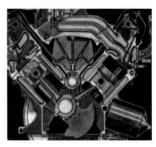

# 1955

Detroit's dreamboats were getting longer and lower as the Fifties progressed, as the Montclair hardtop below clearly demonstrates. Montclair was Mercury's new premium line, above the Monterey and Custom series. All 1955 Mercurys had a wraparound windshield and deeply hooded headlight bezels that accentuated their sleek profile.

Even entry level Custom models (right) wore a fair amount of glitter. Montclair models boasted exclusive trim touches such as bright rocker panel trim and a clever two-tone color swatch beneath the side windows. Mercury sales hit a record 329,000-plus.

# 1956

Mercurys got extra flash for '56 with jazzy Z-shaped side trim. "Flo-Tone" paint schemes were offered in a rainbow of sherbetlike pastel hues. Mercury V-8s grew to 312 cubic inches and could put out up to 235 hp. Like most U.S. automakers, Mercury upgraded to 12-volt electrical systems to handle the stronger starter motors needed for high-compression engines and increased loads from power accessories.

THE VILLAGE SH

# 1957 DREAM-CAR DESIGN

Mercury raced into 1957 with all-new styling and more power, plus a longer wheelbase and new engineering features. Gadgetry abounded— "Keyboard Control" pushbutton controls were now standard with Merc-O-Matic automatic transmission. The new-for-'57 Turnpike Cruiser models offered a "Seat-O-Matic" memory seat with 59 positions, a "Monitor Control" instrument panel with tachometer and trip tally clock, and a special steering wheel flattened at the top.

# STRAIGHT OUT OF TOMORROW
# 1957 Mercury

Though dual headlights were not yet legal in all 50 states, "Quadri-Beam" headlamps were standard on Turnpike Cruisers and optional on other Mercurys in 1957. Rear fenders had unique concave coves which could carry two-tone paint colors on Montclairs and Montereys, or gold-anodized trim on Turnpike Cruisers.

Turnpike Cruisers also featured Breezeway Ventilation, which utilized air intakes at the top of the windshield and a power-retracting rear window for passenger-compartment air circulation. Their outlandish styling and gimmicky accessories made the '57 Mercurys a high point in Fifties kitsch, and a monument to the excesses of the era.

# 1958

New-for-'58 Mercury Park Lane models offered "more than 18 feet of quiet comfort— contoured in distinctive styling." All 1958 Mercurys wore bulkier bumpers and reconfigured trim. For die-hard performance enthusiasts, Mercury offered the 400-hp Super Marauder V-8, but recession-wracked buyers were more interested in economy this year. All medium-priced makes suffered a sharp drop in sales; Mercury's output was off over 40 percent this year.

# 1959

Mercury celebrated its 20th anniversary with bigger cars riding a four-inch-longer wheelbase. The United States was just a few years away from putting a man into space, and space-age design cues crept into many consumer products. Mercury's bodyside sculpting now hinted at the shape of a NASA rocket.

Nash's new Rambler compact car debuted for 1950. Rather than compete directly with the "low-priced three" (Ford, Chevrolet, and Plymouth), Nash management wisely choose a unique style of low-priced car. The Rambler's smaller exterior dimensions, unibody construction, and distinctive styling set it apart from its competition, and made it a sales success. Note the side roof rails on this Rambler convertible— they remained fixed for structural rigidity when the top was down.

Nash's streamlined "Airflyte" models were all-new for 1949, and received minor trim changes for 1950. Statesman models were powered by a 184-cubic-inch six that put out 85 horsepower; longer Ambassador models packed a 234.8-cid, overhead valve six with 115 hp. The "Sky-Lounge" interior featured a "Uniscope" instrument cluster and a pull-out drawer-type glovebox. Both Ambassador and Statesman offered club coupe, two-door sedan, or four-door sedan body styles.

# *1951*

The 1951 Nash Airflyte models were updated with a new vertical-bar grille and squared-up "Sky-Flow" rear fenders with vertically mounted taillights. Ambassadors got extra wraparound chrome trim. Nash was a pioneer of unibody construction, adding unibody cars to its lineup in 1941. Where most American autos utilized a body-on-frame construction, all the major structural elements of a Nash—the entire body and frame, girders, pillars, floor, and roof—were joined by over 8000 welds into a single unit.

Nash's powertrain lineup didn't change for '51. Shown top to bottom at right are the Ambassador's 115-hp overhead-valve six, the Statesman's 85-hp six, and the Rambler's "Flying Scot" 82-hp six. Nash cars excelled in both performance and economy; the company boasted that a '50 Ambassador had traveled 712 miles at 95.3 mph in the Pan American Road Race in Mexico, and a '51 Rambler averaged an impressive 31.05 mpg in the '51 Mobilgas Economy Run.

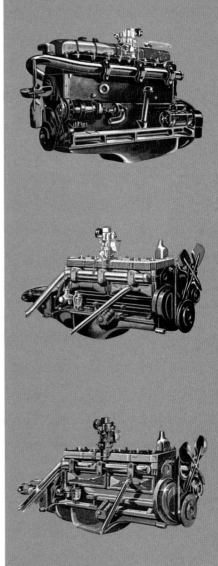

1952

Statesman Country Club

244

Nash's "Golden Airflyte" models were redesigned for 1952, the marque's 50th anniversary year. All-new bodies featured a more squared-up look and a wraparound rear window. Nash's integral front fender skirts, as on the 1949-51 Airflytes, made for large turning circles and difficult tire changing. The Rambler line gained two-door wagon and hardtop models for '51, and continued mostly unchanged for '52. Every Nash was now available in hardtop form; Nash called its hardtop models "Custom Country Clubs."

The 1953 Nashes were virtually identical to the '52s—about the only external difference between them was a series of chrome slats added to the fresh-air intake on the cowl. The standard Ambassador models continued to use a 120-horsepower "Super Jetfire" 232.6- cubic-inch six. Optional was a 140-horsepower "LeMans Dual Jetfire" six with dual carburetors, higher compression, and an aluminum cylinder head.

# 1954

For '54, Nashes were facelifted with a concave grille and new headlight bezels. A Continental spare tire was now standard equipment on Custom models. This ad illustrates one of Nash's more unusual features: fold-down seats that formed a twin-bed-sized sleeping area. Times were getting tough for independent automakers, and some joined forces to survive. Nash-Kelvinator and Hudson Motor Car Co. combined to form American Motors on May 1, 1954.

1954 Nash Ambassador Custom Four-Door Sedan, photographed in scenic Arizona.

## New!

## Nash Year-'round Air Conditioning Costs Hundreds of Dollars Less!

Now you can own the finest car on the road today—a Nash with *year-'round Air Conditioning*—for less than most *un-equipped* cars. Yes, Nash has something entirely new—the world's first combined *cooling-heating-ventilating* system. Keeps you cool in summer, warm in winter—*automatically*—filters out dust and pollen all year long.

See your Nash dealer's amazing demonstration of the new "All-Weather Eye" Air Conditioning System today—available on even lowest-priced Nash Ramblers.

**1** **Recline and travel relaxed!** Nash Airliner Reclining Seats beat anything you ever tried for travel comfort. Either front seat back adjusts to any of five relaxing positions.

**2** **Not a single inch** of wasted trunk space with Nash Air Conditioning. And the continental outside tire mounting (standard on Custom models) adds extra luggage room.

**3** **You're free to sleep** anywhere—be first on the spot when the fish start biting—in your Nash with Twin Beds. Form-fitting mattresses and insect screens available.

**4** **Good news at the gas pump!** You'll go farther on a gallon than you ever dreamed possible.

**5** **Enjoy the Best** eye-level visibility. Try optional Power Steering, Power Brakes, Power-Lift Windows, Hydra-Matic.

## Nash Airflytes

AMBASSADOR · STATESMAN · RAMBLER · METROPOLITAN

BUILT WITH A "DOUBLE LIFETIME" . . . YOUR SAFEST INVESTMENT TODAY . . . YOUR SOUNDEST RESALE VALUE TOMORROW

# 1955

Nashes were facelifted for '55 with a wrap-around windshield, a new oval grille encircling the headlights, and two-tone side trim. The Nash-Healey sports car was built in limited numbers from 1951-55.

1956

Nashes were mildly facelifted for 1956 with more chrome trim and available three-tone paint, as shown on this Ambassador Special Country Club hardtop. Ambassador Specials held the new 250-cid Torque-Flo V-8. Improved Flashaway Hydra-Matic transmission promised "whip-quick response." Despite the upgrades, model-year production plunged by two-thirds.

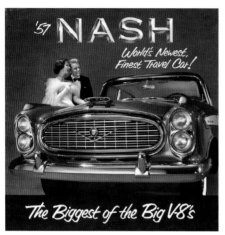

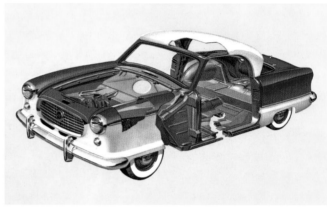

The 1957 facelift brought Nashes dual headlights, a new grille, and revamped side trim. Sales were still miserable, and the full-size Nash was dropped after a minuscule production run of less than 3600 cars. With the demise of the Nash and Hudson lines, American Motors focused more on its small-car offerings, such as the Rambler and the diminutive Metropolitan. Though Nash was gone, the Ambassador name lived on, returning as a 1958 line of stretched Ramblers.

The British-built Nash Metropolitan two-seater debuted in 1954 in hard-top and convertible form. An improved Metropolitan, the 1500, was introduced in mid 1956. The 1500 monicker referred to the metric displacement of a 90.9-cid Austin four churning out 52 horsepower, 24 percent more than the old "1200." Styling was updated with a mesh grille and zigzag side moldings that delineated loud two-tone paint schemes.

Oldsmobiles were at the leading edge of automotive style and engineering in 1950. Bodies had ultramodern one-piece windshields, and breakthrough overhead-valve V-8s were underhood. The "Rocket" V-8s debuted in 1949, and are often credited with starting the "horsepower race" that would escalate through the 1950s.

Oldsmobile's 98 and Super 88 models wore an updated grille design and more bodyside chrome for 1951. As before, the "Rocket" V-8 put out 135 horsepower from its 303.7 cubic inches. The six-cylinder engine was no longer available. At $3025, the 98 DeLuxe convertible was the flagship model.

# OLDSMOBILE

Oldsmobile's Ninety-Eight models were its largest and most expensive, competing at the upper end of the middle-priced car market. GM had carefully organized its divisions into a "stepladder" structure of increasing price and prestige. Cadillac ruled the roost, followed by Buick, Oldsmobile, Pontiac, and Chevrolet.

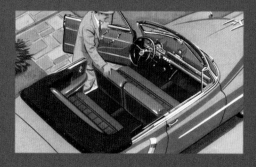

# NEW "ROCKET" ENGINE

Oldsmobiles were little-changed on the outside, but the "Rocket" V-8 got a horsepower boost for '52. Ninety-Eight and Super 88 Oldsmobiles packed a new 160-hp version with a high-lift camshaft and four-barrel "Quadri-Jet" carburetor. Entry-level 88 models got a two-barrel version with 145 horsepower. Power steering was a popular new option that added $185 to the cost of an Olds.

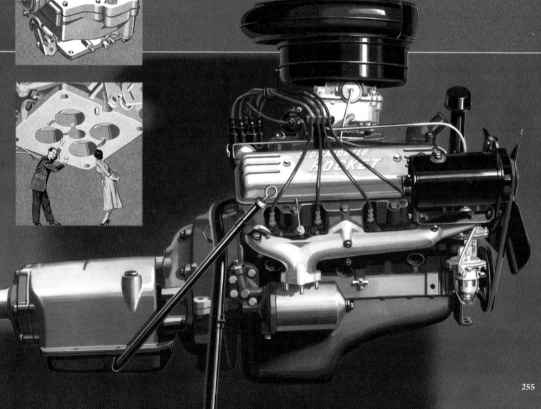

# 1953

The 1953 Oldsmobiles wore a new bumper/grille motif with large oval outriggers on the horizontal grille bar. Again at the forefront of engineering advancement, Oldsmobiles switched from 6-volt to 12-volt electrical systems. The resulting higher voltage meant faster engine starting and more power for accessory equipment. New options for the year included Bendix power brakes ($33) and factory air conditioning from GM's Frigidaire division (a stiff $550). Oldsmobile's rocket was a popular symbol that was frequently utilized in dramatic advertising artwork and stylized chrome trim pieces.

Redesigned 1954 Oldsmobiles (above) wore squared-up bodies with predictive "Panoramic" wraparound windshields and a slightly "dipped" beltline. The famed Rocket V-8 engine was expanded to 324.3 cid. A substantial facelift gave the 1955 Oldsmobiles a bold oval grille, hooded headlights, and jazzier two-toning. "Holiday" was Oldsmobile's name for its pillarless hardtop models; a trendsetting four-door Holiday hardtop body style debuted midway through the '55 model year.

Most American automakers enjoyed a booming year in 1955. Oldsmobile fared especially well, producing its 5-millionth vehicle amid a record-breaking production run of 583,179 cars. An 88 Holiday coupe, shown above in Burlingame Red and white, was the most-affordable Olds hardtop at $2474. The Rocket V-8 was up to 185 horsepower in 88s, or 202 in Super 88s and Ninety-Eights.

1956

The 1956 Oldsmobiles were reworked with updated trim and a mouthy, jet-intake-inspired grille. The Rocket V-8 again got a horsepower boost, this time to 230 horsepower in two-barrel-carbureted versions, and 240 in the four-barrel engine. Dual exhausts were an option for the first time. All Ninety-Eights came standard with a column-shifted "Jetaway Hydramatic" automatic transmission.

The flashy spinner hubcaps
shown on this Lime and
Charcoal Gray 88 Holiday hardtop coupe were popular with
Fifties hot-rodders and customizers. Symmetrically styled
dashboards were a mid-Fifties
Oldsmobile theme that began
with the 1953 models. The round
speedometer and clock faces of
'53-'55 gave way to larger, oval-
shaped designs for '56.

# 1957

Another new body and a larger 371-cid Rocket V-8 were Olds talking points for 1957. J-2 referred to a triple-carburetor performance option that yielded 300 horsepower; a J-2-equipped Olds 88 could do 0-60 mph in less than nine seconds. Station wagon models, absent from the Olds lineup since 1950, returned this year.

TRY THE NEW

# J2 ROCKET

FROM

## OLDSMOBILE

Most exciting engine
development since the first
Rocket was launched

# 1958

*Every window of every Oldsmobile is SAFETY PLATE Glass*

*Right on time! Patti Lewis meets Jerry after work in their new 1958 Fiesta*

**They've discovered**
## OLDSmobility
**...the family-fun way
of going places
in the Rocket Age!**

Get set for a brilliant new way to go places! It's Oldsmobile's versatile new Super 88 Fiesta . . . the car with something for everyone *and more*! Slim, sleek lines make it smart as the handsomest hardtop! Interior luxury is as elegant as the finest town car! Yet it's roomy and rugged . . . ready for any load or road . . . and powered by the thrilling new Rocket Engine. Discover *OLDSmobility* in the fullest, most exciting sense of the word! See and drive a glamorous new Super 88 Fiesta by Oldsmobile, new! OLDSMOBILE DIVISION · GENERAL MOTORS CORPORATION

*See THE JERRY LEWIS SHOW · Tuesday Night, April 15 · NBC-TV*   KEEP YOUR HEADLIGHTS AIMED RIGHT

## OLDSMOBILE

Gaudy, bright-work-drenched styling earned 1958 Oldsmobiles the nickname "Chromesmobiles." The trademark wide oval grille was gone, replaced by a bulky bumper design and heavily trimmed quad headlights. The red tanks shown below are air chambers for "New-Matic Ride," Oldsmobile's version of GM's ill-fated air suspension. The systems offered negligible gains in ride quality and were notoriously unreliable.

1959

264

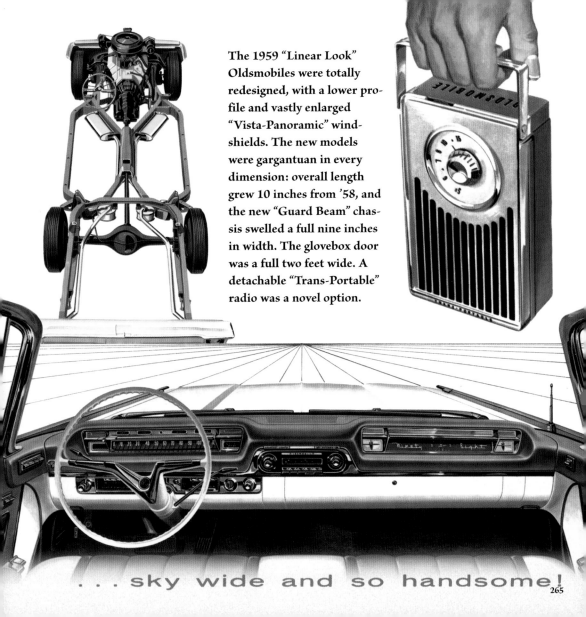

The 1959 "Linear Look" Oldsmobiles were totally redesigned, with a lower profile and vastly enlarged "Vista-Panoramic" windshields. The new models were gargantuan in every dimension: overall length grew 10 inches from '58, and the new "Guard Beam" chassis swelled a full nine inches in width. The glovebox door was a full two feet wide. A detachable "Trans-Portable" radio was a novel option.

. . . sky wide and so handsome!

Packard entered the Fifties with a mild facelift of its bulbous "bathtub" models, which debuted in 1948. Three trim levels were offered, all with straight-eight engines: Eights had a 135-horsepower 288-incher, Super Eights had a 150-hp 327, and Custom Eights packed a 160-hp, 356-cid engine. Packard's Ultramatic automatic transmission, which debuted in mid 1949, was standard on Customs, optional on others.

Impressive and award-winning a few years earlier, Packards now seemed painfully portly, and were often derided as "pregnant elephants." Sales plunged from 116,248 in 1949 to just 42,627 in 1950.

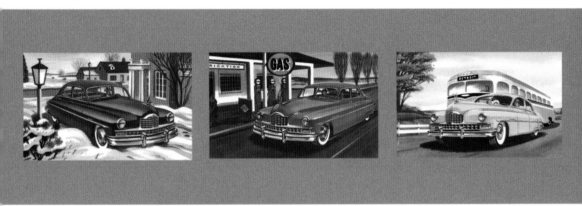

# 1951

Packards gained a modern, squared-off profile in their 1951 redesign. Model designations were new as well—the Packard line now consisted of 200, 250, 300, and Patrician 400 models. The sole ragtop was the $3391 250 convertible. The entry-level 200 series included a $2616 DeLuxe Touring Sedan and, in stark contrast to the ultraposh Packards of the past, a stripped-down Business Coupe for $2302.

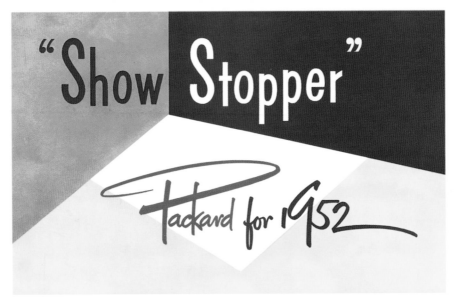

# "Show Stopper"

*Packard for 1952*

For '52, Packard styling went virtually untouched, but power brakes arrived as a first-time option. Packard's line-topping Patrician 400 four-door sedan sold for $3797, and wore exclusive trim with four chrome bodyside "scoops." Packard's top "Thunderbolt" inline eight produced 155 horsepower from its 327 cubic inches.

Packards for 1953 and '54 were again little-changed except for the expected trim updates and a stronger focus on luxury models. For '53, the Clipper nameplate was revived for Packard's junior models, and the former 300 and 400 models were renamed Cavalier and Patrician. Packard merged with ailing Studebaker in late 1954 to form the Studebaker-Packard Corporation.

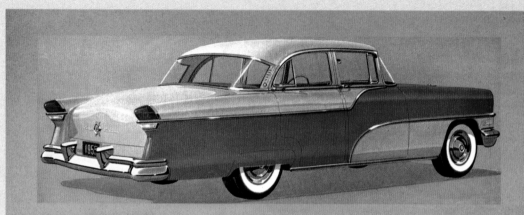

# 1955

The 1955 Packards wore an extensive facelift of the old '51 body. Styling updates included "cathedral" taillights, peaked front fenders, an ornate grille, and that '55 must-have, a wraparound windshield. Clippers gained their own special grille and retained 1954-style taillights. Packards finally ditched their antiquated straight eights in favor of all-new V-8s; the limited-edition Caribbean's 352-cid V-8 put out 275 horsepower.

# 1956

Packards were facelifted again for 1956, the last year that "true" Packards would be sold. Clippers were now marketed as a separate make, but sales continued to flounder. The company was sinking fast, being pulled down with Studebaker.

# 1957

Although the revered Packard name lingered on for 1957, it now identified a Studebaker clone. Only two models made the lineup: a four-door sedan selling for $3212, and a $3384 Country Sedan wagon. New-car shoppers were not fooled by this sad charade—less than 5000 '57 Packards were sold.

# 1958

Packards were again based on Studebakers for 1958, this time exhibiting a hasty restyle with tacked-on quad headlights and tailfins. The Packard Hawk (shown) was an awkwardly restyled luxury version of the Studebaker Golden Hawk. It packed a supercharged 289-cid V-8 that put out 275 horsepower. Packard production for 1958 sunk even lower than 1957's already dismal levels. The once-proud marque suffered an ignominious end midway through the season, as Studebaker-Packard announced a halt to Packard production.

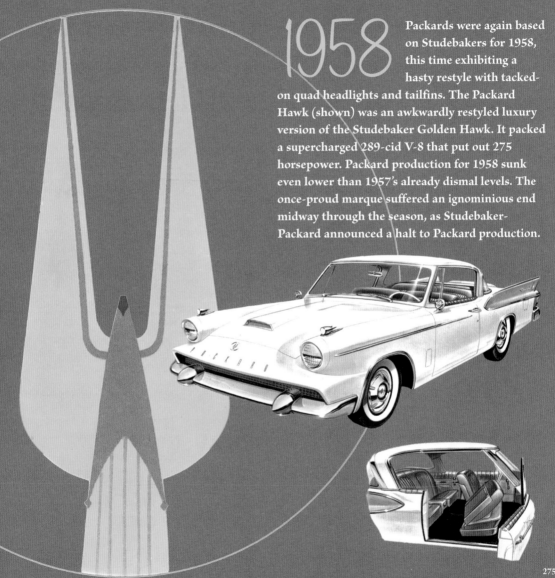

The 1950 Plymouth line was basically a reprise of the new-for-'49 models. An effective facelift brought a simpler square grille with a large horizontal bar, slightly longer rear decks, and taillights placed low within reworked fenders. Plymouth's new Suburban steel-sided station wagons could look drab, but they caught on quickly. The extra cost and special maintenence requirements of real-wood-bodied station wagons would spell their demise—Plymouth offered its last "woodies" this year.

The 1950-52 Plymouths were powered by a 217.8-cubic-inch inline six that made 97 horsepower. The 1951 and nearly identical '52 models gained a modified hood and a lower, wider grille that made frontal appearance a little less blunt. In the above ad, Plymouth chose to illustrate the benefits of its "Solex" safety glass by picturing a camel wearing a hat.

# 1953

The 1953 Plymouths got an outer-body reskin that brought flow-through fenderlines, a one-piece windshield, and a more-aggressive grille. Streamlined hood ornaments used a stylized *Mayflower* ship motif.

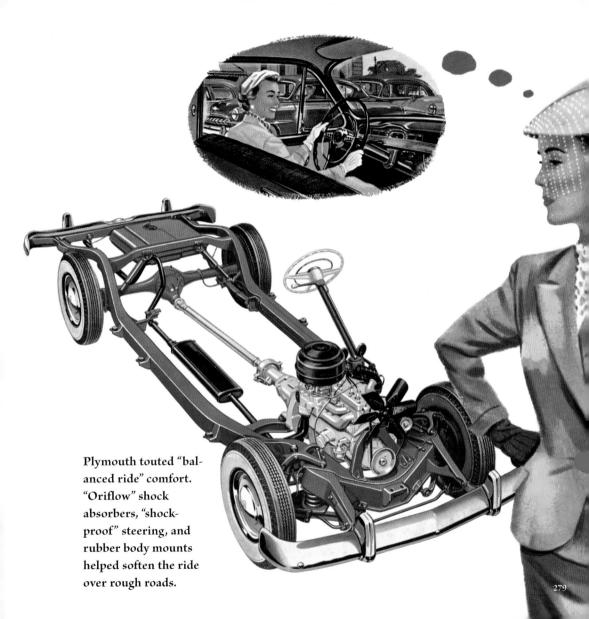

Plymouth touted "balanced ride" comfort. "Oriflow" shock absorbers, "shockproof" steering, and rubber body mounts helped soften the ride over rough roads.

279

# 1954

The 1954 Plymouths were mildly facelifted with a glitzier grille, thicker headlight bezels, and more chrome all around. Belvedere models sprouted tiny chrome fins on their rear fendertops. Optional wire wheels and Continental spare-tire kit added extra flash.

The Plymouth model line expanded for 1954, with three new series names: Plaza, Savoy, and Belvedere. During the model year, Plymouth's six-cylinder engine was enlarged to 230 cubic inches and its output rose to 110 horsepower. Two-speed PowerFlite, Plymouth's first fully automatic transmission, also appeared midseason.

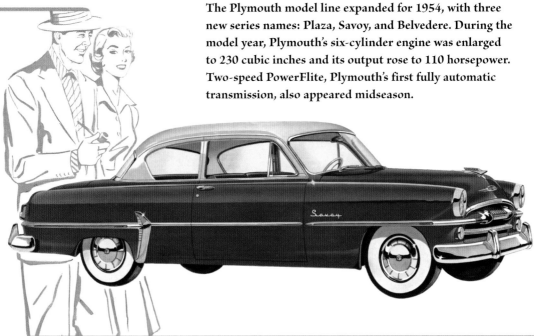

# 1955

Plymouths were redesigned for 1955, with crisp new styling and the division's first V-8 engine. The "Hy-Fire" V-8 packed 167 horse-power in base form, 177 hp with the "PowerPak" option. Belvederes could get dramatic "Sportone" two-tone finishes.

# 1956

PUSH·BUTTON

NEW *PowerFlite*

POWER

PLYMOUTH '56

The 1956 Plymouths got a revised grille, updated trim, and bigger tailfins. PowerFlite automatic-transmission-equipped cars now had pushbutton controls. Bigger "Hy-Fire" V-8s now put out 180 horsepower in base form.

POWER FOR SAFETY!

283

# 1957

Plymouths were all-new, and radically different, for 1957. Bodies were much lower and wider, with distinctive "shark" fins and a graceful grille. Plymouth ads proclaimed, "Suddenly, it's 1960"— and not without reason. Next to its rivals, Plymouth really did seem "three full years ahead," with the lowest profile and the highest tailfins of its low-priced competition. Earlier in the decade, Plymouth had struggled with the stodgy image of its vehicles, but the new '57s obliterated that problem. Production shot up over 200,000 cars, to 762,231.

NEW OBSERVATION SEAT available in 9-passenger Plymouth Sport and Custom Suburbans. More legroom. Folds flush into floor for extra cargo space.

*from the Observation Seat of your*

# BIG, NEW PLYMOUTH SUBURBAN

*see how far behind the "other two" are*

Here's a dazzling new *kind* of station wagon . . . the big Plymouth Suburban! 3 full years ahead! With exciting new features you can't get on any other station wagon in the field!

Just a few of the many important advances are shown on the opposite page. You enjoy them in the biggest . . . longest . . . widest . . . roomiest station wagon in the low-price 3.

In fact, you can't buy bigger at any price! 12 exciting models. 2-door and 4-door. New, higher-power six and terrific new FURY V-8 engines—super-powered up to 290 hp!

# 1958

Plymouth stayed at the forefront of Detroit's horse-power race with its limited-edition Fury models, which debuted in 1956. For '58, the Fury packed a potent "Dual Fury V-800" 318-cubic-inch V-8 with 290 horse-power, or an optional 350-cid "Golden Commando" 350-cid V-8 that put out 305 hp.

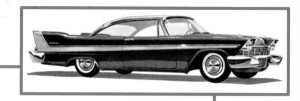

A mild but attractive 1958 facelift brought Plymouths quad headlights, round taillights, and slightly revised trim. Top-line Belvederes wore a full-length trim spear that could feature a two-tone color swatch or brushed-aluminum trim. Midlevel Savoy models could have a two-tone color sweep on the lower rear fenders and doors. A Belvedere Sport Coupe cost $2457.

# 1959

The 1959 Plymouths wore a heavy-handed restyle, with longer and higher fins, and a garish eggcrate grille. The Fury name was expanded into top-line Fury and Sport Fury models. A "Sport Deck" simulated spare-tire cover graced the decklid of Sport Furys. Swivel seats were standard on Sport Furys, optional on other models.

## IF IT'S NEW, PLYMOUTH'S GOT IT!

NEW SPORT DECK standard on SPORT FURY models shown above . . . available at slight extra cost in every Plymouth price range.    * Optional, extra cost

### ANNOUNCING THE '59 PLYMOUTH    Brings you new beauty, new features, and new FURY

models at a new low price! Plus a new standard of performance with the New Golden Commando 395 Engine * !

At Plymouth dealers now: Today's best buy...tomorrow's best trade!

'59 Plymouth

**YOU ENJOY NEW SWIVEL SEATS** that make '59 Plymouth Sport Fury the easiest car to get in and out of. Front seats swing smoothly with you as you enter or leave. New Plymouth exclusive in the low-price field!

**YOU GET INSTANT HEAT** at finger-tip touch with new Push-Button Heating and Ventilating Controls *. No waiting for warmth on frosty mornings in '59 Plymouth! Teams with Plymouth's magic Push-Button Drive *. All buttons conveniently grouped in an impressive new Master Control Center handy to your reach.

**YOU AVOID GLARE** as new electronic Mirror-Matic rear-view mirror * automatically dims headlight dazzle from cars behind. A great new safety advance.

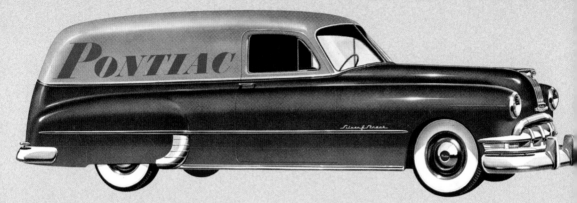

The 1950 Pontiacs were largely carried over from the all-new-for-'49 models, but got revised trim, a fresh grille, and a new two-door hardtop body style called Catalina. The 1951 models (bottom left and right) got a new V-motif grille, flashier bodyside trim, and a new rear decklid handle/emblem.

Other than a mild retrimming, Pontiacs were little-changed for '52. Broad "Silver Streak" chrome hood and trunk trim was a Pontiac tradition dating back to 1935. As in 1950-51, both 239.2-cubic-inch straight-six- and 268.4-cid straight-eight engines were available. Both engines could get an automatic transmission, GM's improved "Dual-Range Hydra-Matic."

# 1953

Pontiacs were heavily revamped for 1953, with longer bodies and one-piece curved-glass windshields. The Chieftain Custom Catalina hardtop wore a "Panoramic View" wrap-around rear window. Power steering was newly optional.

# 1954

AIR OFF
TEMP OFF        LOW

Nineteen fifty-four brought a minor facelift of 1953's major one. Rearranged side moldings and a narrow oval in the central grille bar were the main changes. The big news was Star Chief, a top-line eight-cylinder hardtop (shown), convertible, and four-door sedan on a new longer chassis.

Pontiac claimed its 1955 models were "new in everything but Pontiac's great name!" Lower-profile bodies featured contemporary styling touches such as a wraparound windshield and two-tone-friendly bodyside trim. Star Chief models were again the flagship series, followed by Chieftain 870 and base Chieftain 860 models.

Pontiac's stalwart straight-six and straight-eight engines were now gone forever—under 1955 Pontiac hoods lurked a brand-new overhead-valve "Strato-Streak" V-8. In standard form, the 287.2-cubic-inch engine put out 173 horsepower with manual transmission or 180 with automatic; an optional four-barrel carburetor yielded an even 200 hp.

# 1956

## superb new beauty

The 1956 Pontiacs were mildly restyled, with a bolder, chromier grille and revised bodyside two-toning. Pontiac wagons shared body panels with their Chevrolet siblings, but camouflaged them with unique taillights and trim. A Chieftain 870 Catalina hardtop coupe, shown below in Vista Blue and Chesapeake Blue, went for $2480.

The "Strato-Streak" V-8
grew to 316.6 cid, and
made 205 horsepower in
Chieftains and 227 hp in
Star Chiefs. At midyear, a
hotter dual carburetor 285-
hp version was produced in
limited numbers. Star
Chief models had smoother
shifts, thanks to the "all-
new, power-smooth Strato-
Flight Hydra-Matic trans-
mission."

1957

Pontiac closed out its successful "Strato-Streak" generation with facelifted 1957 models. The high-performance Bonneville convertible debuted with a fuel-injected 310-hp V-8—and a whopping $5782 price tag. The specially-trimmed La Parisienne four-door hardtop (below) was a one-off show car.

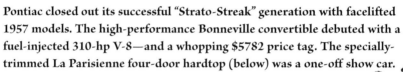

# 1958

Unlike some 1958 GM cars, Pontiac's restyle was reasonably tasteful, with a simple mesh grille, quad headlights, and side spears made wider and concave toward the rear. A 370-cid V-8 was now standard across the board, delivering up to 285 horsepower in Star Chiefs and Bonnevilles.

All 1958 Pontiacs featured asymmetrically patterned interiors in a wide variety of two- and three-tone color combinations. Model offerings now included no fewer than seven Catalina hardtops with two or four doors. New Pontiac gadgetry for '58 included a removable "Sportable" transistor radio, a "Safeguard" speedometer that buzzed when a driver-set speed was exceeded, and a "Memo-Matic" power seat that moved rearward for easier entry and exit when the ignition key was turned off.

1959

300

Pontiacs were completely new for '59. Crisp styling on all-new bodies featured minimal side trim and modest twin fin rear fenders, and introduced Pontiac's trademark split-grille theme. New "Wide Track" engineering increased tread width by nearly five inches, greatly improving stability.

## Rambler

All-new Rambler models were introduced for 1956, and wore Nash or Hudson badges. Four body styles were available: four-door sedan, four-door hardtop, four-door wagon, and an industry-first four-door hardtop wagon. Reshuffled trim and available V-8 power were added for 1957, when Rambler became a make of its own.

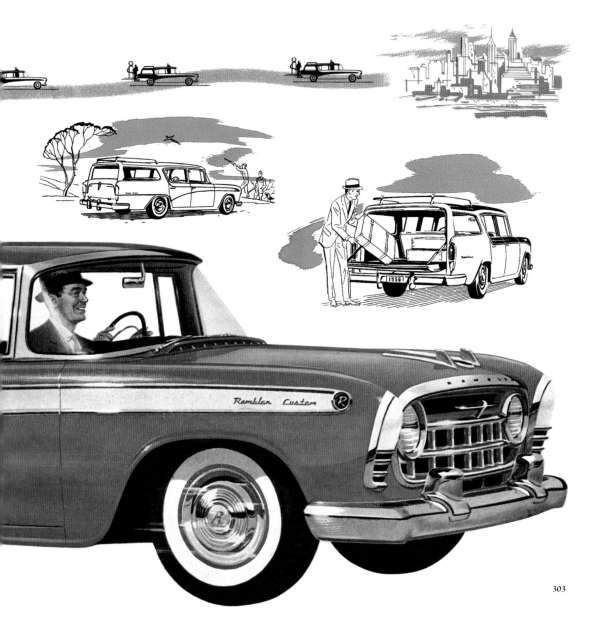

303

For 1958, American Motors took the unusual step of reviving its 1955-vintage Rambler. Except for a new grille and enlarged rear wheel openings, it looked like the three-year-old model upon which it was based. Now badged as the Ramber American, the cars arrived at an opportune time: during a recession, as compact imports were capturing serious sales.

Only one American body style was offered, a two-door sedan. Underhood was a 90-horsepower, 195.6-cubic-inch six-cylinder, or as the Rambler American brochure christened it, a "World-famous Super Flying Scot Engine!" It promised up to 30 miles per gallon, which was important to a growing number of economy-minded shoppers. Ford, General Motors, and Chrysler all took note of the increasing popularity of small economy cars, and began developing compact cars of their own, but wouldn't have competitive models ready until the 1960 model year.

# STUDEBAKER

Dramatic "bullet-nose" front-end styling appeared on Studebakers for 1950. Exterior appearances changed little for '51, but V-8 power was newly available. Starlight coupes wore a distinctive wraparound rear window

Studebaker's 232.6-cid,
120-horsepower V-8 was
the first overhead-valve
V-8 from an independent
automaker, and the first
in the low-price field. The
V-8 came standard in
top-line Commander
models; Champion mod-
els got a 169.6-cubic-inch,
85-horsepower six.
Styling was freshened for
1952 with a low and
toothy full-width grille,
and a new Starliner pil-
larless hardtop coupe
body style was added to
the model lineup.

The all-new-for-'53 Studebakers boasted a low-slung, European look. Wonderfully styled by Robert Bourke of the Raymond Loewy studio, the '53 Studebakers are widely considered a landmark of modern design. Eggcrate grille inserts identified the little-changed '54 models. Also new for '54 were seven extra horses for Commander models, larger brakes across the board, and a two-door Conestoga station wagon body style.

A chrome-heavy facelift marked 1955 Studebakers. Flashy two-tone color schemes and new side trim brought more glitz, and a de rigueur wraparound windshield was added on some models at midyear. The top engine option for the year was a 259.2-cid V-8 with 185 horsepower.

# 1956

Studebakers got a squarer, more-upright look for 1956, with a large, mesh-filled grille. The $2529 President Pinehurst was the top station wagon model. Each President model carried a 289-cid V-8, rated 195, 210, or 225 hp.

*Craftsmanship with a flair!*

Studebaker's gutsy 1956 Golden Hawks packed a 275-hp, 352-cid V-8 borrowed from corporate partner Packard. Just 4071 were produced, with a $3061 price tag. Golden Hawks were based on the original 1953 "Loewy coupe" design, but updated with modest tailfins and a large square grille riding high on an elevated hood.

Studebaker's financial woes dictated only modest restyling for 1957 and '58. A restyled grille and taillights marked the '57s; 1958 models got clumsy tailfins and tacked-on quad headlights. For the ultrafrugal, Studebaker offered drab, decontented Scotsman models with six-cylinder power and very little chrome.

# 1959

Studebaker enjoyed sudden success with its new-for-'59 Lark models. The compact Lark replaced Studebaker's standard line—and more than doubled the company's sales. Two-door hardtops, sedans, and wagons were offered, along with a four-door sedan. Golden Hawk models were dropped, leaving a lone Silver Hawk coupe with six-cylinder or V-8 power.

# Aero-Willys

After a successful stint building Jeeps for World War II, Willys-Overland reentered the American passenger-car business with the 1952 Aero-Willys models. Fashionably square and slab-sided, the Aero-Willys was relatively light, roomy, and blessed with good handling. Entry-level Aero-Larks used a 75-horsepower, 161-cid six-cylinder, while uplevel models ran an overhead-valve "Hurricane" six with 90 hp. Model offerings expanded for 1953, but appearance changed only in detail—notably red hubcap emblems and a gold-plated "W" in the grille.

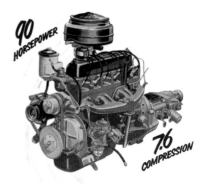

90 HORSEPOWER

7.6 COMPRESSION

# WILLYS HAS

Four-door sedans were added to the Aero-Willys lineup for 1953. Hydra-Matic automatic transmission joined the options list late in the model year. Topping the line was the $2157 Aero Eagle hardtop coupe; the $1646 Aero-Lark was the most affordable model.

# everything*

\* Visibility

\* Roominess

and \* Unmatched Economy

In 1953, Willys-Overland was pur-
chased by Henry Kaiser, who combined
it with ailing Kaiser-Frazer to form
Kaiser-Willys Sales Corporation. Aero-
Willys were little-changed in outward
appearance for 1954, save for hooded
headlight bezels and larger taillights.
The Kaiser 226-cid six-cylinder engine
became available in Aero-Willys models
in March 1954, upping the top horsepower rating from 90 to 115.

The 1955 Willys line received an ambitious facelift with a handsome new grille, fresh side trim, and larger taillights with integrated back-up lights. Despite the updated look, sales continued to plummet. Kaiser-Willys decided to abandon the U.S. car market by early 1955.

# Cars
# Produced
# in the 1950s

| | | |
|---|---|---|
| 1. | Chevrolet | 13,419,048 |
| 2. | Ford | 12,282,492 |
| 3. | Plymouth | 5,653,874* |
| 4. | Buick | 4,858,961 |
| 5. | Oldsmobile | 3,745,648 |
| 6. | Pontiac | 3,706,959 |
| 7. | Mercury | 2,588,472 |
| 8. | Dodge | 2,413,239* |
| 9. | Studebaker (U.S.) | 1,374,967 |
| 10. | Packard ('50-'58) | 1,300,835 |
| 11. | Chrysler | 1,244,843* |
| 12. | Cadillac | 1,217,032 |
| 13. | Nash ('50-'57) | 974,031* |
| 14. | DeSoto | 972,704* |
| 15. | Rambler ('57-'59) | 641,068* |
| 16. | Hudson ('50-'57) | 525,683* |
| 17. | Lincoln | 317,371 |
| 18. | Kaiser ('50-'55) | 224,293* |
| 19. | Henry J ('51-'54) | 130,322* |
| 20. | Edsel ('58-'59) | 108,001 |
| 21. | Imperial ('55-'59) | 93,111 |
| 22. | Willys ('52-'55) | 91,841 |
| 23. | Continental ('56-'58) | 15,550* |
| 24. | Frazer ('50-'51) | 13,914* |

\* Includes calculated or estimated figures

DB HK TK